Crucial

9 Sessions on
Prayer
for
7 to 11's

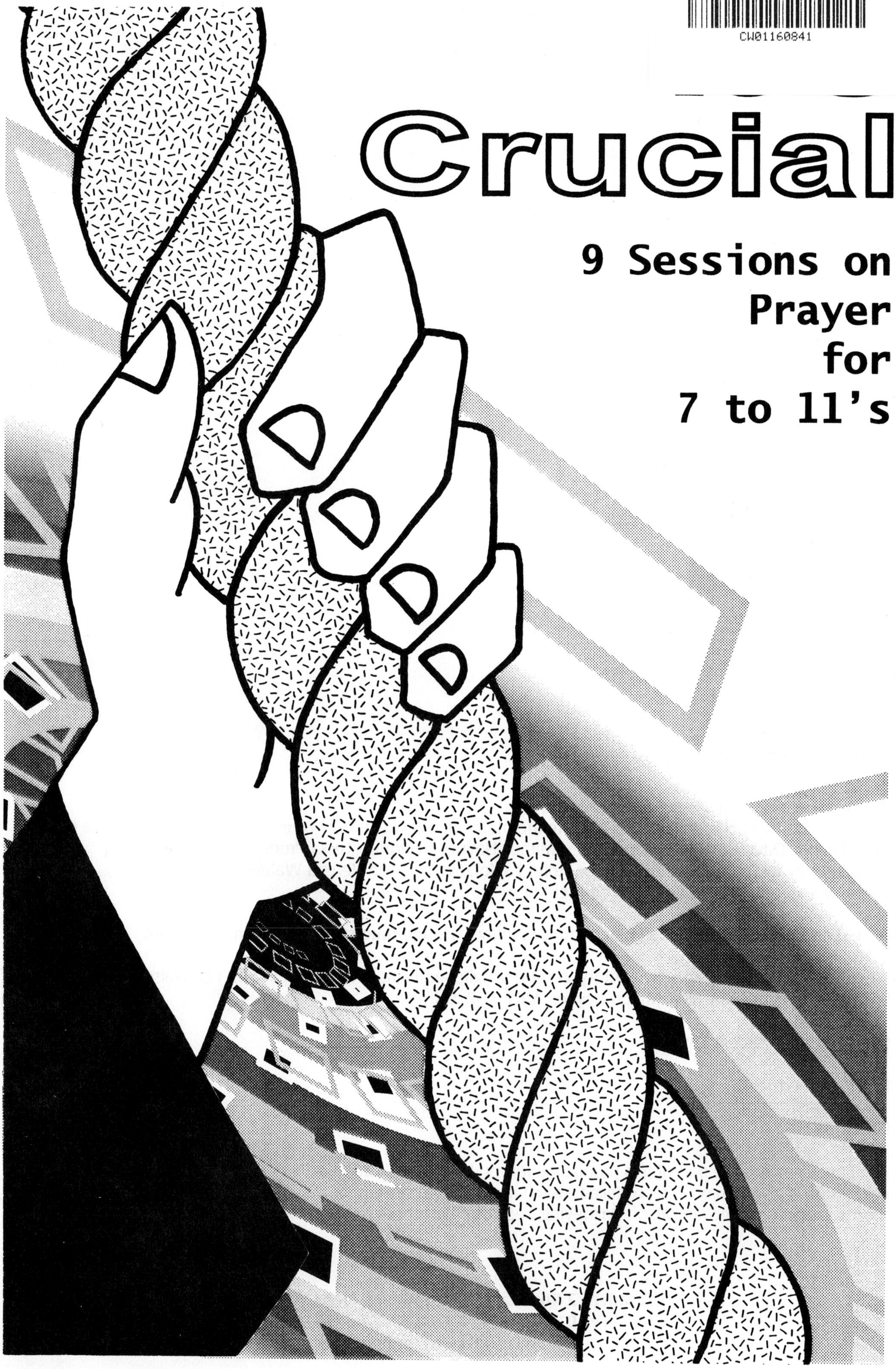

ACKNOWLEDGEMENTS

It's Crucial was originally devised by Hilary Creed;
Hilary Creed and Elaine Williams then wrote the material, with help from Teresa Brice, Liz Doré, Joanne Gale, Dave Fowler, Dave Glover, Miriam Harvey, Manus Hayne, Liz Potter, Tessa Prodger, Millie Purdy, Margaret Reynolds, Margaret Rhys-Tyler, Anne Taylor, Lindsey and Verena Walder;
Matthew Slater did the artwork and typesetting.

Printed and bound in the United Kingdom by Stanley L. Hunt (Printers) Ltd., Rushden, Northants.

Scriptures quoted from the New Century Version (Anglicised Edition) copyright © 1993 by Nelson Word Ltd, 9 Holdom Avenue, Bletchley, Milton Keynes, MK1 1QR, UK.

Copyright © Crusaders 1997

First Published 1997

ISBN 1 897987 10 2

All rights reserved. No part of this production (other than the children's activity sheets for which specific permission is given) may be reproduced, stored in a retrieval system, or transmitted in any form or by any means, electronic, mechanical, photocopying, recording or otherwise, without the prior permission of Crusaders.

Crusaders, 2 Romeland Hill, St Albans, Herts, AL3 4ET.
Tel: 01727 855422, Fax: 01727 848518;
E-mail crusaders@ukonline.co.uk

Contents

Introduction iv
A Few Words about our Approach to Prayer vi
Learning to Pray - Step by Step vii
Guidelines for Prayer Supporters xi

iii

Introduction

When did you last use a length of rope? To tow the car, hang out the washing ...or for something more spectacular? With confidence in the strength of rope we can fall from the sky and scale mountains. And rope can save lives...

Using rope as an illustration, *It's Crucial* aims to help your children increase their understanding and experience of prayer, however limited that experience might currently be! Given the opportunity, children can pray naturally and with real trust. Prayer makes space for communication between a child and God... that's why it's so exciting!

Each session in *It's Crucial* follows the same pattern:

THE FIRST PAGE is a session overview for <u>you</u> and develops the rope theme. To involve and interest your children in the theme, you could:

- give each child a piece of string 50 cm long and challenge everyone to include it in a picture to show rope being used - this would be a good activity (or competition) before beginning the series!

- make a visual aid for the series: fix a length of rope (or similar) as near to the ceiling as possible - make sure it's within reach of your children! Attach things to the rope as you go through the sessions, eg prayers, pictures, key verses...

- have a competition to see who can guess the rope 'picture' before you begin each session - but give clues!

You will also find a **prayer point** on this page, which offers you specific guidelines for prayer in your leadership team. (All of these **prayer points** have also been reprinted on page xi for you to photocopy and send to your prayer supporters.)

The teaching material is then divided into three sections:

The most important section, including:

- **Set the Scene** - an activity to introduce the theme and prepare your children to learn...

- **Present the Bible Base** - suggestions for telling the story;

- **Focus...** - guidelines to help you help your children think about the crucial points;

- **Pray!** - guidelines for your prayer time (to be used with **Learning to Pray - Step by Step** on pages vii to x. Do make sure that you leave plenty of time for this!

Two more learning activities, including:

- **Prayer Notes** - a very simple prayer journal to help your children record the main points from the teaching session and what they have prayed.

[You could slot these activities, as appropriate, between the different parts of the Crucial section, eg Set the Scene, Present the Bible Base, Quiz, Focus..., Prayer Notes, Pray!.]

Three optional activities which link in with or build on the theme. We have suggested at the end of each one how you could tie it in with the teaching content.

> **To help your children get the most out of these activities:**
>
> - make sure you have all the materials and equipment to hand before you start... enthusiasm is easily lost if you keep children hanging around while you get organised!
>
> - have a non-scoring practice run before actually playing a game;
>
> - always be clear and consistent when awarding points or applying rules... fairness is very important to children of this age - it is never 'just a game' to them!
>
> - try to make an example of each craft activity to show... this will help your children visualise what they themselves could produce! And you will be better able to lead the activity if you've already done it yourself;
>
> - make a point of encouraging every child... not just those who are successful and good at the activity.

You will also find some **Additional Ideas** at the end of many sessions, which tend to need a bit more advance planning... we suggest that you look through now to see if you want to use any of them in your group!

[You could run the activities in this section before or after (or before and after!) the Crucial material. Also, if you don't like Set the Scene in any session, you could use one of these activities instead - but don't choose anything which will make it difficult for your children to concentrate afterwards...]

> As always, please remember that you will certainly need to tailor the material in *It's Crucial* to suit the needs and interests of your unique group of children!

A Few Words about our Approach to Prayer...

We all bring to any teaching on prayer our own understanding and experience, which is partly determined by our Church background. In preparing *It's Crucial*, we have assumed that:

- just as Jesus welcomed the children who were brought to him, so He will welcome the children in our groups who step towards him in prayer. This welcome is not dependent on the spiritual status of the child;

- God will answer the sincere prayer of any child, (but we may need to help them see that He does not always say 'yes');

- encouraging our children to express their needs in prayer and trust God for help is a valid starting point for a relationship with him... Many people first came to Jesus because they wanted or needed something and recognised that He had the power to help;

- our main aim is to get our children to pray. (On balance, it's better to let children pray things which are important to them, but which might seem inappropriate to us, than to leave them so concerned about what to pray that they do not pray at all!)

We have tried to make *It's Crucial* neutral on certain key prayer issues... it's up to you to to add 'flavour' according to your own convictions!

> **Pray in the Spirit at all times with all kinds of prayers...**
> *(Ephesians 6:18)*

Learning to Pray - Step by Step

In each session we provide a *prayer topic* and a *visual prayer focus* based on the Bible story... But it's up to you to decide how to actually pray with your children! Here is a step-by-step approach: we suggest you try to identify where your children would be most comfortable <u>now</u>, then seek to move them on as you go through this series.

But please remember:

➤ that our aim is to give our children the freedom and stimulus to pray themselves... we may well not see all of this happen over the course of 'It's Crucial', but we can certainly make steps towards it!

➤ to be sensitive to your children... start small, and don't rush or pressurize them;

➤ that these steps are only guidelines... don't feel constrained to follow them like a set of instructions and feel free to add other ideas you come across!

➤ that prayer is not about finding the right formula or strategy... it's about relationship;

➤ to let God dictate the pace as He works in the lives of the individual children in your group!

'Raising Awareness'

YOU simply make YOUR CHILDREN aware that YOU are praying for them ~

Note down the specific needs mentioned by your children in each session and pray about them.

Modelling Prayer

YOU pray short, simple and specific **prayers on behalf of** YOUR CHILDREN ~

1) <u>In groups</u> - Ask your children to be quiet and to close their eyes - do not be afraid to wait for them to do this! Then,
either pray about anything mentioned by individuals during the session - it is wise to ask their permission for this first...
or pray about things you know to be relevant to children of this age! We suggest you keep your eyes open whilst you're praying so that you can make eye contact with any children who find it difficult to concentrate!

2) <u>As individuals</u> - Offer opportunities to pray with children on their own... BUT BE WISE! If possible, do this in a corner of the meeting room with your backs turned to the others. If you really need to go somewhere else to pray, make sure you are visible the whole time and that other leaders know where you are. Also, know what action to take if a child discloses something serious to you.

... And Getting them involved!

YOU frame a prayer, leaving space for YOUR CHILDREN to talk to God themselves ~

A prayer for session two, for example, might go something like:

> 'Dear God, thank you that you promise to help us through hard times. The things which we find hard are........ [QUIET] .... Please help us, Lord. Amen.'

You can develop this over a number of sessions, by leaving longer spaces!

YOU pray, YOUR CHILDREN join in by repeating a single line ~

A prayer for session five, for example, might go something like:

YOU:	Thank You, God, for our families -
EVERYONE:	*Thank You, God!*
YOU:	Thank You, God, for the food we eat -
EVERYONE:	*Thank You, God!*

...and so on.

YOU 'create' the prayers, YOUR CHILDREN pray them ~

'Create' one or two **short, simple and specific** prayers in advance - write them out in lower case lettering and clear, print-style handwriting **or** as a mixture of words and picture cues. Then:

▶ have everyone say the prayers altogether;

▶ ask for volunteers to read them aloud.

[Please help those who are less confident readers to be involved in this kind of prayer activity by reading through the words before you all pray them!]

YOU carefully choose Bible prayers or Psalms, YOUR CHILDREN pray them ~

We have not specifically included the Lord's Prayer (*Matthew 6:5-15*), for example, but you may well want your children to pray it as part of this series. You might like to:

▶ write out the prayers **or** Psalms and have everyone say them altogether;

▶ ask for volunteers to read them aloud.

[Please help those who are less confident readers to be involved in this kind of prayer activity by reading through the words before you all pray them!]

YOU provide a published book of prayers, YOUR CHILDREN choose and pray them ~

Borrow or buy a good book of prayers for children such as *365 Children's Prayers*, by Carol Watson (Lion); *The Lion Book of Children's Prayers*, by Mary Batchelor (Lion); *My Own Book of Prayers*, by Mary Batchelor (Lion).

Show the book to a small group of children and simply let them choose a prayer (or prayers!). Then:

▶ have everyone say the prayers altogether;

▶ ask for volunteers to pray them on behalf of everyone in the group.

[Please help those who are less confident readers to be involved in this kind of prayer activity by reading through the words before you all pray them!]

Creating and Rehearsing Prayer

YOUR CHILDREN 'create' their own prayers, YOU help ~

Ask your children to write **or** draw their own short prayers on separate pieces of paper - you could have different coloured paper for different kinds of prayers! If appropriate, stick these prayers to the visual focus for the session. Then:

▶ ask for volunteers to pray some of the prayers on behalf of everyone in the group;

▶ have individuals pray their own prayers.

[Please help those who find writing difficult by letting them dictate their prayers to you!]

YOUR CHILDREN make their own book of prayers, YOU help ~

Have each child design his/her own page, which could include:

▶ their own written prayers;

▶ drawings of people and situations they would like to pray about;

▶ pictures cut out of magazines of people and situations they would like to pray about;

▶ prayers copied from good published collections for children of this age - (please see the previous page for recommendations).

Keep these pages together in an attractive loose-leaf folder. Have individuals choose a different page to be used as a prayer focus each session.

[Please help those who find writing difficult by letting them dictate their prayers to you!]

Praying more freely

YOUR CHILDREN pray in a round, YOU begin a 'chain' ~

For session five, for example, you could begin: 'thank you God for .....'. As you go round the circle, each child adds another item **or** repeats the phrase 'thank you God for .....' and adds his/her own ending. Say 'Amen' altogether after the last contribution!

[Reassure your children that it does not matter if two or more pray the same thing! And be prepared if some children laugh at what others suggest: explain that God is interested in everything that matters to us.]

YOUR CHILDREN pray in a round, YOU provide the 'cue' ~

Give one of the children in the circle an object (eg a Bible)... he/she prays a short prayer and passes the object to the next person, who then prays **or** just passes the object on... and so on round!

[Reassure your children that two or more can pray about the same thing! Please don't let anyone feel under pressure to pray out loud, but encourage everyone to join in with the 'Amen' at the end!]

YOUR CHILDREN pray in a round, YOU provide the 'prompts' ~

In advance, get together different objects **and/or** pictures relating to the theme: for session six, for example, have items to remind your children of the different people's needs, (eg for an elderly person: a brown envelope (= bills, money worries), a picture of one unhappy person (= being lonely), a tin of food (= help with shopping) etc.) Give each item to a child **or** small group of children. Bring out how each item reminds us of something a person needs, then encourage your children to pray!

ix

YOUR CHILDREN pray for each other in a round ~

Ask your children to get into pairs (**or** threes). Ask everyone to ask their partner what he/she would like prayer for. Perhaps also encourage them to think of something good about that person to thank God for. Then have your children stand in a circle and pray round...!

[Be aware of the state of relationships in the group - children who have fallen out with each other will find this prayer activity hard!]

YOU invite YOUR CHILDREN to say short, unrehearsed prayers on behalf of everyone else ~

You might begin with volunteers: ask first who would like to pray out loud. Say each volunteer's name to let them know it's their turn to pray! Give an opportunity for anyone else to pray before ending the session. Over time you can lead on to more 'open', less-structured prayer sessions...

YOUR CHILDREN pray together ~

Simply ask your children to get into pairs **or** small groups to pray!

YOUR CHILDREN pray! ~

Ask your children to choose one (or more!) of the people or situations mentioned in the session, then to continue praying about them during the week...

YOUR CHILDREN grow in their understanding of prayer as communication in relationship with God Himself, YOU continue to teach, guide and support ~

▶ help your children establish a 'place of prayer' for themselves - somewhere to go regularly to spend time with God;

▶ help your children listen to God and discern what He is saying;

▶ introduce the concept of 'arrow prayers' (- prayers we can say very quickly when we don't have time for a conversation with God, eg *Nehemiah 2:4!*):

Help your children think back over their day: when could they have shot 'Thank You' or 'Please' prayers up to God? Perhaps have two different coloured arrows - one for 'Thank You', one for 'Please'. Ask your children to write 'arrow prayers' on them. Then write 'GOD' on a board **or** wall **or** poster-sized piece of paper - have your children stick their 'arrow prayers' anywhere, as long as they point to God!

▶ look deeper into the prayers in the Bible, especially 'The Lord's Prayer' (*Matthew 6:5-15*):

For example, from the 'Your will be done' line, get your children to talk about what God might think of a particular situation: can they remember what Jesus said about this ...and so on. Then pray! This would introduce our need to fit in with what God wants and also the fact that He helps us know what to pray...

▶ help your children make and keep a 'prayer journal';

▶ check out *You too Can Change the World* by Daphne Spraggett and Jill Johnstone (OM).

▶ contact organisations such as YWAM for details of 'Daniel Prayer Groups' and accompanying resources.

Dear

Please would you join with us in praying for our group as we go through our next teaching series?

Guidelines
for Prayer Supporters

---

1. Date:
Nehemiah 1:1-2:8

Nehemiah prayed and waited for the resources he needed... What resources are needed for the work in your group - more leaders? more time? greater prayer support? something else...? PRAY about these... Working with children can seem daunting at times, so ask God for the kind of faith which helped Nehemiah face his massive task...!

2. Date:
Nehemiah 2:11-20 and 4:1-23

Sanballat and Tobiah tried to intimidate Nehemiah and his team... PRAY especially for any children in your group who are being bullied in any way: ask God to keep them safe and protect them in mind, body and spirit... PRAY that they will have people who love and value them.

3. Date:
Nehemiah 6:1-16

Nehemiah did not give up despite considerable opposition... PRAY especially for children in your group with specific problems at the moment: that God would give them all they need to keep going and grow through them... PRAY also for any who seem to give up trying very easily.

4. Date:
Daniel 2:1-49

Daniel knew where to look for answers... Nebuchadnezzar certainly did not!! PRAY against the subtle influences which will already be telling our children that God is just one of many options: ask God to reveal His true self to them!

5. Date:
Daniel 3:1-30

It would have been easy for Shadrach, Meshach and Abednego to go along with the crowd... and our children also face pressure to do (or not to do) what everybody else seems to be doing. Ask God to give them the courage to stand up for what they know to be right! PRAY that the pressure to conform will not stop them making their own decisions about God.

6. Date:
Daniel 6:1-28

Clearly, prayer was no empty ritual or chore for Daniel... Ask God, by His Spirit, to water the seeds of a desire to meet with Him in the hearts of every child in your group. Also, PRAY especially for children from not-yet-Christian homes: that they would be able to find space to spend time with God.

7. Date:
Matthew 19:13-14 & 26:36-39; Mark 1:35 and Luke 6:12-13.

Jesus showed us what it means to be in relationship with the Father... and then made it possible for each of us to enjoy this relationship ourselves. PRAY that each child will really hear this... Ask God to draw each child to Jesus (John 6:44).

8. Date:
Luke 7:36-50

The woman was acutely aware of her own sin and immensely grateful for the love and forgiveness Jesus showed her... Ask God, by his Holy Spirit, to gently help your children see their need to own up and be sorry (John 16:8-9), and then to know how good it is to be forgiven!

9. Date:
Matthew 26:36-46

Jesus died for us. PRAY for each child in your group by name: that he/she will really understand this. And use one of Paul's prayers: "I pray to God that (...) every person listening to me today would be saved..." (Acts 26:29)

Thank You!

1 Nehemiah

LEADERS OVERVIEW

Take a deep breath... jump... count down... pull the rip cord! Parachutes are often used to get people and relief supplies into needy situations. And the tiny rip cord is always absolutely crucial!

Nehemiah might have liked a parachute and a pack of supplies! He enjoyed a good life as the cupbearer to the king of Persia himself, yet Nehemiah's heart was in Judah, his homeland. In 446BC, he learnt that Jerusalem's walls were in ruins and his people in great difficulty... it was devastating news, but what could he do? Nehemiah poured out all his unhappiness to God and prayed for help. And then he waited for God's answer...

Three months later, King Artaxerxes asked Nehemiah what was troubling him. Nehemiah prayed first before answering. That short prayer was like a parachute rip cord: Nehemiah was given permission to go to Jerusalem and promised resources to start building... God was launching him into the biggest adventure of his life!

We would all love easy and instant answers to our prayers. Nehemiah's experience reminds us that God always answers prayer... but we may have to wait and we may be part of the answer!

Nehemiah prayed and waited for the resources he needed... What resources would help you work more effectively with the children in your group - more leaders? more time? greater prayer support? something else...? PRAY about these... And if working with your group seems daunting at times, ask God for the kind of faith which helped Nehemiah face his massive task...!

We Would Like Our Children to...

... know that we can always talk with God about things which are important to us.

Key Verse

First I prayed to the God of Heaven.
Nehemiah 2:4

Bible Base

Nehemiah 1:1-2:8
(Nehemiah's Prayer to Nehemiah is Sent to Jerusalem)

It's possible to deliver most of the material in these three sessions through groupwork. If you would like to do this - and have helpers who can lead small groups - perhaps develop the 'superheroes' idea and name the groups after current heroes. You could also have a team competition, make 'superhero' badges, decorate each area of your meeting room...

Set the Scene

In advance, find one or two pictures of current 'superheroes' (eg Superman, Batman...) in comics **or** magazines. Tack them in obvious places around your meeting room before your children arrive!

1. Have everyone sitting in their small groups **or** in one large circle.

2. Give everyone a piece of paper and a pen **or** pencil.

3. Draw attention to the 'superheroes' around the room and ask your children to name some others.

4. Explain the activity: **'we are going to invent some new superheroes! To start with, what does a superhero look like? Just draw a superhero's head and face on the paper, but leave room for other things...!** (pause for drawing time!) **...Now give your picture to the person on your right. What does a superhero wear? Draw some clothes on the picture you have now!'**

   [Each superhero picture is a combined effort, so no-one feels under pressure to produce one on their own!]

5. Continue building up the pictures with questions such as: **'what does this superhero do? How does this superhero travel about? Where does this superhero live? What special power does this superhero have?'** ...and so on.

6. Allow time to look at and talk about the superheroes your children invent.

You will need:
some 'superheroes'!
Blu-tack
paper
pens **or** pencils

Present the Bible Base

Option A: Cartoon Strip

In advance, make copies of the cartoon strip version of the Bible story on page 7 - enough for one each.

Simply help your children get to grips with the story! Ask them to draw the expression on the blank face marked * - then talk together about how Nehemiah must have felt.

You will need:
to make copies
pens **or** pencils

Option B: Dramatic Presentation

You will need:
to practise!

In advance, work out a short drama, using the cartoon strip version of the Bible story on page 7 as the script!

Perform the drama! Involve your children by asking them to say how Nehemiah must have felt - and then have that acted out - as suggested in the cartoon strip version.

Focus...

<u>Either</u> in small groups <u>or</u> altogether, ask questions to bring out the main points, such as:

➤ *What made Nehemiah sad?*

➤ *Do you think Nehemiah was a 'superhero' to start this job?!?*

[Help your children grasp of the hugeness of Nehemiah's task: rebuilding the walls of an entire city!!! If possible, try to give them an idea of the scale of the project by comparing the distance with something they know - the total length of the walls was about 2km.]

➤ *Who did Nehemiah go to for help?*

[Your children will probably say the king first... but bring out clearly that Nehemiah went to <u>the King</u> first!!]

Pray!

You will need:
cups
notepaper
pens <u>or</u> pencils

In advance, choose <u>how</u> you want to pray from **LEARNING TO PRAY** (pages vii to x). Also, get together some cups to act as a reminder of Nehemiah and prayer-prompt - try to find something more associated with wine than tea or coffee! Perhaps decorate some paper cups yourself to make them look slightly more fit for a king, <u>or</u> set this up as an activity for children who arrive early. You will need one cup for each prayer group.

1. <u>Either</u> in small groups <u>or</u> altogether, ask: ***what have you been thinking a lot about this week?*** Draw out what is important to your children at the moment - this might be something fun (eg a holiday or a birthday) <u>or</u> something difficult (eg a family problem or concern about someone who is unwell). You may wish to note these down as you go along...!

   [Please don't press anyone for an answer!]

2. Remind your children about Nehemiah's prayers by saying something like: ***'Nehemiah was thinking a lot about the city in his homeland which was in ruins, so he talked with God about it. He asked God for help and waited for God's answer. Just like Nehemiah, we can talk with God about the things which are important to us - and, just like Nehemiah, we must be ready to wait...'***

3. **NOW PRAY!** Base your prayer-time on the idea you have chosen from pages vii to x. Use the cups as appropriate, eg:

   ● offer the cup to a child. Ask him/her to say what he/she is thinking a lot about at the moment. Then pray! Pass the cup round and do the same for other children;

cont'd....

- give everyone a small piece of paper and a pen **or** pencil. Ask them to write **or** draw whatever they are thinking a lot about at the the moment and add their name... but explain that you will look at it afterwards! Collect all the pieces of paper in the cup. Take them out, one by one, and pray!

Prayer Notes

In advance, guess how many children will be coming to your session, divide the number by two and make that many copies of page 8! Fold the copies widthways along the dotted line. Make holes at each side with a hole-punch - if you centre this with the full line, you should end up with holes over the small crosses! Now cut along the full line to separate the two sheets. Also cut lengths of string of about 35cm - enough for one per child.

You will need:
to prepare the 'prayer notes'
string
coloured pens **or** pencils

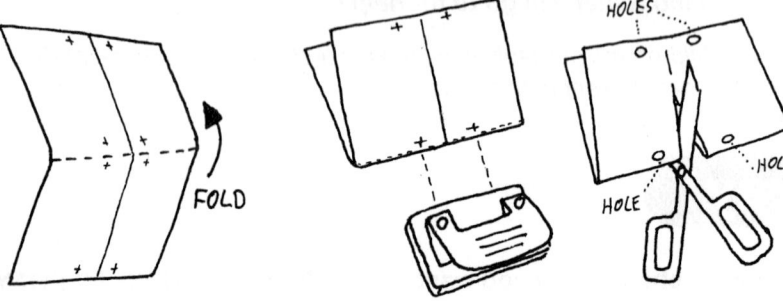

1. Give each child one of the folded 'prayer notes' and a length of string.

2. Ask your children to do the puzzle, colour the picture and complete the key verse on the other half of the sheet.

3. Also, ask your children to think of **something which is really important to them now...**

4. ...Ask them to write about this **or** draw it inside their 'prayer notes'.

5. Finally, ask your children to thread the string through the two holes and tie it at the front - explain that this will mean that what they write inside will be kept secret between them and God!

[The string will also reinforce the rope theme and help you keep each child's prayer notes together!]

Answers:
1. permission
2. letters
3. timber
4. soldiers

Extra Activities

SUPPLY RACE

You will need:
a collection of 'supplies'
a strong carrier bag with handles
a length of rope
a stopwatch

You may need:
small prizes!

In advance, get together as many things as you can to represent 'supplies' of any kind (eg empty food and drink containers, bandages, wood, nails...).

1. Ask your children to get into two equal-sized teams - A and B.

   [If each team is bigger than eight, we suggest that you run two (or more!) supply races, so double up as necessary!]

2. Have team A stand at one end of your meeting room with the supplies... then position team B a distance away with the carrier bag. Run the rope between them.

3. Explain the game: *'imagine that team B really needs these supplies! Team A can get them over to team B, but there is a dangerous river between you, which nobody can cross. To start with, team B needs to thread the bag onto the rope and get it quickly over to team A on the other side. When the bag arrives, team A can put one thing into it and send it back. Be careful not to let the supplies touch down! We will time you to see how quickly you can do it...!*

4. Run the game, ensuring that everyone has a turn holding the rope.

   ALTERNATIVE IDEA:
   A challenge! Mark out the river (which cannot be crossed). Give team A the supplies and carrier bag and team B the rope... see if your children can work out how to get the supplies from team A to team B. Set a time limit, if you'd like to add a bit more tension!

 **To Tie This in:**

Team B had to rely on team A for supplies ~ Nehemiah knew he could rely on God for all he needed... and so can we! Rope linked the two teams ~ prayer links us with God.

VIDEO QUIZ

You will need:
to prepare this!

You may need:
paper
pens **or** pencils
small prizes!

In advance, choose a five-minute video clip of a 'superhero' in action! Think of up to ten questions about the clip.

1. Have everyone sitting in their small groups **or** ask your children to get into teams of about six.

2. Simply show the video clip... but explain beforehand that there will be questions about it afterwards!

3. Now ask the questions!

cont'd.....

4. The team with the most correct answers, wins.

 **To Tie This in:**

This superhero can do amazing things because he/she has special powers ~ Nehemiah was able to do something amazing because God gave him power through prayer! The superhero's powers are not real ~ God's power is!

MODEL PARACHUTES

In advance, cut the material _or_ polythene into 20cm squares and the sewing cotton into 20cm lengths - you will need one square of material and four lengths of cotton for each parachute! Also, do some of the stages below if your children are likely to find the whole thing a bit much!

You will need:
to prepare!
material **or** polythene
strong sewing cotton
pipe cleaners

You may need:
scraps of material
scraps of wool
scissors
glue
a picture of a
   parachutist

1. Make the parachutist first - if you have time, clothe the parachutist with scraps of material and give him/her some hair!

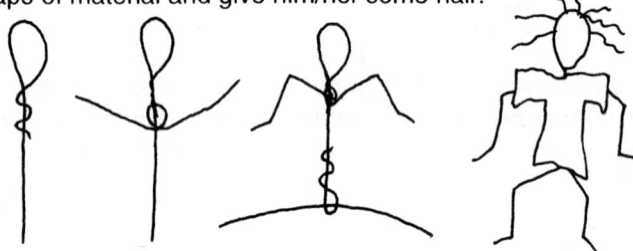

2. Tie a length of cotton to each corner of the square...

3. ...Then tie all four lengths of cotton to the parachutist.

4. Allow time to launch the parachutes and see how they work!

 **To Tie This in:**

Do your children know how a parachute works in real life - and what it is used for? Nehemiah's short prayer was a bit like pulling the tiny rip cord on a parachute: as he prayed, God 'launched' Nehemiah into the most exciting adventure of his life with all the resources he needed to start the job!

ADDITIONAL IDEAS:

1. Parachute games are great fun and would fit in well with this session! Get hold of a parachute and some games ideas!

2. 'Party Poppers' also have short 'rip cords'! You could have your children pop some to illustrate the teaching point above... but please supervise this carefully! With some groups, you could even use 'party poppers' as part of the prayer time...!

The Adventures of Nehemiah - Part 1

✱ Draw in here how you think Nehemiah might have looked.
Remember his hair, eyes, ears and mouth!

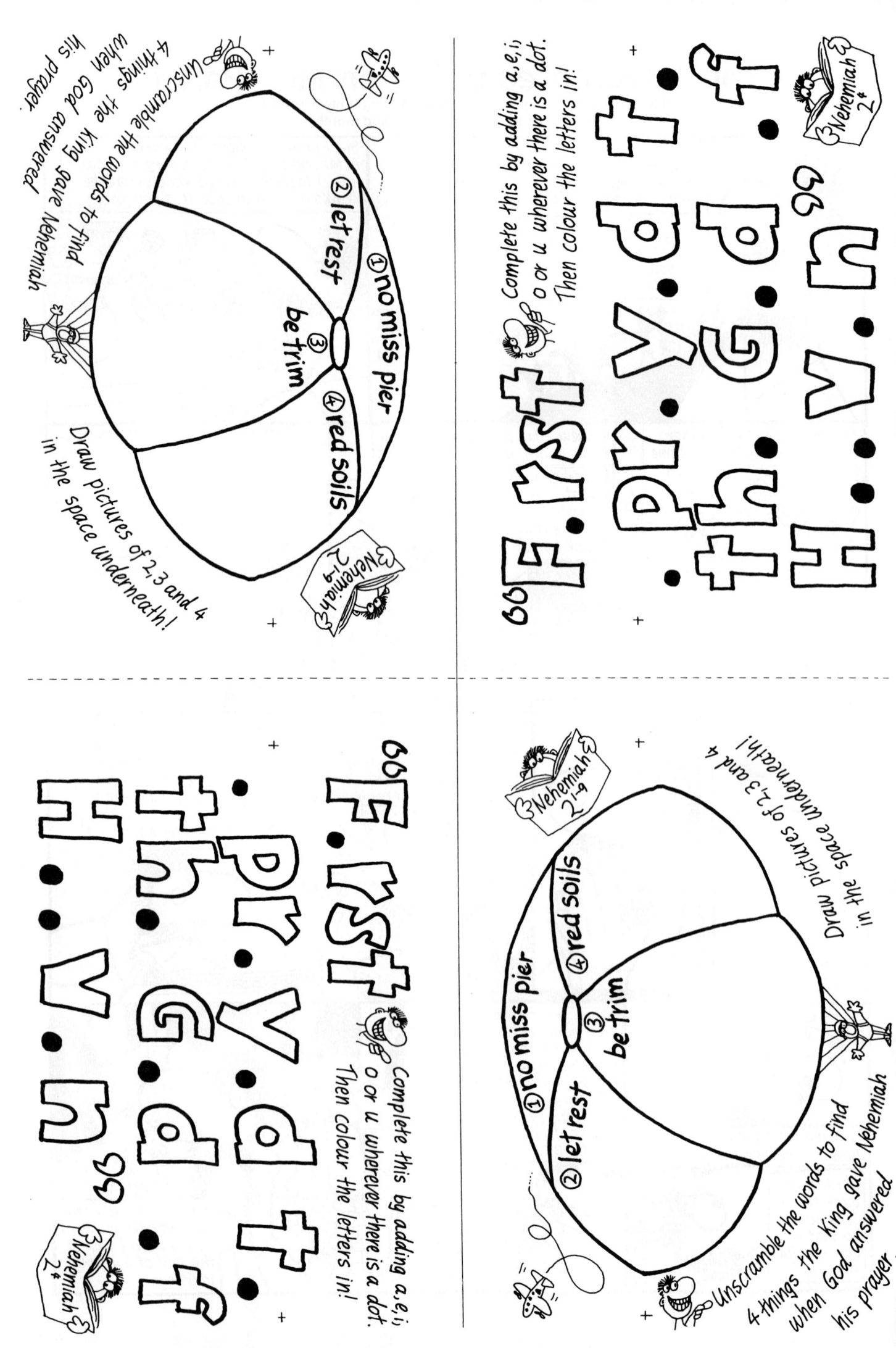

2 Nehemiah

LEADERS OVERVIEW

From the bottom of a sheer rock face, we might wonder how anybody could ever make it to the top... But with the right equipment - including rope - the mountaineer learns to overcome each separate challenge to climb higher.

There were plenty of challenges awaiting Nehemiah in Jerusalem. Not only was he faced with the huge task of rebuilding the walls, but there were also people determined to try and stop him. Nehemiah met every problem with prayer and, trusting in his faithful God, refused to let anybody stand in his way.

It's tempting to ask God to smooth out the difficulties in our lives, but He often seems to prefer to use them for good, strengthening our faith as we grow to trust him more and more. We might prefer a 'leisurely stroll', but God often seems to offer a strenuous and challenging 'climb'!

Let's encourage our children to pray about the problems they face: God may not make them disappear, but He will help them through!

Sanballat and Tobiah tried to intimidate Nehemiah and his team... PRAY for any children in your group who are being bullied in any way: ask God to keep them safe and protect them in mind, body and spirit... PRAY that they will have people who love and value them.

We Would Like Our Children to...

... see that God helps us meet the challenges in our lives through prayer.

Key Verse

[Nehemiah said:] "Don't be afraid of them. Remember the Lord, who is great and powerful."
Nehemiah 4:14

Bible Base

Nehemiah 2:11-20 & 4:1-23
(Nehemiah Inspects Jerusalem **and** Those Against the Rebuilding)

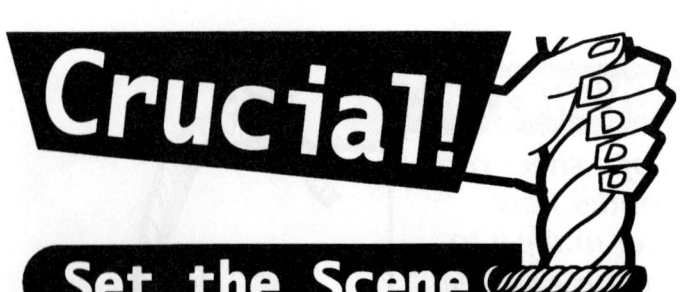

Crucial!

Set the Scene

In advance, think of a number of challenging situations which your children could easily relate to (eg being bullied, starting a new school, going to the dentist...) - but don't make them too 'heavy'! Write each situation on a separate piece of paper - you will need one per group.

You will need:
to think of some situations

1. Have everyone sitting in their small groups **or** ask your children to get into groups of about six.

2. Give one situation to each group to develop into a short drama...

3. ...After a few minutes, stop the action and explain: **'now turn your play into a human cartoon strip! Have four 'pictures' in your cartoon strip. Remember, people in cartoon strips don't move and they don't talk!'** Help your children work out how to show what is going on with facial expressions and 'frozen action'.

   [Of course, there can be movement between each 'picture'!]

4. Have an opportunity to see each 'cartoon strip' - ask the rest of the group to guess what is going on before moving on to the next one.

   [You may want to begin to talk together about possible solutions to these problems, but there is a Part Two to this activity... please see HELP! in the EXTRA ACTIVITIES section.]

Present the Bible Base

Option A: Cartoon Strip

In advance, make copies of the cartoon strip version of the Bible story on page 15 - enough for one each.

You will need:
to make copies
pens **or** pencils

Simply help your children get to grips with the story! Also, ask them to draw people building the wall in the picture marked *.

Option B: Dramatic Presentation

In advance, work out a short drama, using the cartoon strip version of the Bible story on page 15 as the script!

You will need:
to practise!

Perform the drama! Involve your children by asking them to act out building the wall, as suggested in the cartoon strip version.

Focus...

Either in small groups or altogether, ask questions to bring out the main points, such as:

➤ *What did the troublemakers do to try and stop the re-building work?*

[Help your children recall that the troublemakers made fun of Nehemiah and then threatened to attack. Perhaps then ask your children to talk about a time when someone made fun of them or threatened to hurt them...]

➤ *What did Nehemiah do about this?*

[Highlight the fact that Nehemiah **talked with God first... then did something** about it! If possible, also tell your children simply and briefly about a challenging situation God helped you through. As appropriate, help your children explore how following Nehemiah's example could work out for them in real life.]

Pray!

You will need:
to make some bricks!
pens or pencils
Blu-tack

In advance, choose how you want to pray from LEARNING TO PRAY on pages vii to x. Also, make some 'bricks': cut out rectangles, roughly the same size, from suitable-coloured paper or card.

1. **Either** in small groups **or** altogether, remind your children about Nehemiah's prayers by saying something like: *'when things got tough for Nehemiah, he knew he could rely on God for help. God wants us to talk with Him about the things which are hard for us too* (give examples, perhaps linking with SET THE SCENE), *and He wants to help...'*

2. Ask: *are you finding anything hard at the moment? Or do you know anyone who is having a tough time?* (Again, perhaps give examples...)

3. **NOW PRAY!** Base your prayer-time on the idea you have chosen from pages vii to x. Use the 'bricks' as appropriate, eg:

   ● make a 'prayer wall' for anyone (including group members) in tough situations at the moment. Write each name and situation on a separate 'brick' and tack them together. Keep the 'prayer wall' going: move 'bricks' to one side as issues are resolved... invite your children to add 'bricks'... Use your 'prayer wall' over coming weeks as a visual reminder that God answers prayer!!

Extra Teaching

Key Verse

You will need:
to prepare!

In advance, collect together about eight 'blocks' (eg cardboard boxes, empty cereal and washing powder cartons...). Cover the surface of each 'block' and write part of the KEY VERSE on it, large enough for everyone to see.

1. With your children altogether, bring out the 'blocks' (but not in order, of course!).

2. As a whole group, work out the right order for the 'blocks' and build them into a 'wall'.

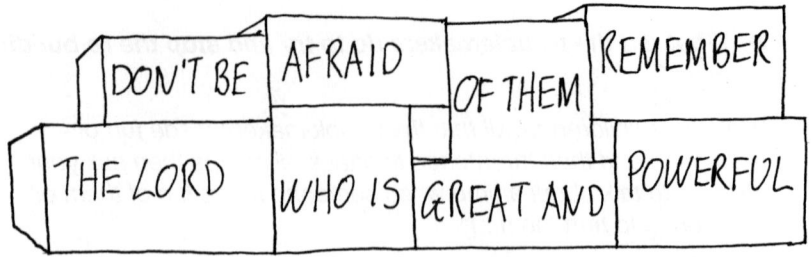

3. Help your children learn the verse by turning round (**or** carefully removing!) a 'block' at a time and seeing if they can remember what was on it!

Prayer Notes

In advance, prepare the 'prayer notes' on page 16 - see page 4 for guidance!

1. Give each child one of the folded 'prayer notes'.

2. Ask your children to do the puzzle, colour the picture and complete the key verse on the other half of the sheet.

3. Also, ask your children to think of *any things they (**and/or** anyone known to them) are finding hard at the moment...*

4. ...Ask them to write these things **or** draw pictures of them inside their 'prayer notes'.

5. Finally, ask your children to add this session's 'prayer notes' to the first by threading the string through the two holes and tying it at the front.

You will need:
to prepare the 'prayer notes'
coloured pens **or** pencils

Answers:
The things Nehemiah faced were: a hard job; something he'd never done before; people making fun; enemies waiting to attack.
*He overcame them with **prayer** and **trust in God**.*

Extra Activities

NIGHTLINE!

In advance, set up an obstacle course around your meeting room *or* building, *or*, if possible, use the natural obstacles in a nearby park or wooded area! Run the rope securely round and over the obstacles.

1. Blindfold a child and give him/her the beginning of the rope...

2. ...Set him/her off round the obstacle course, using the rope as a guide!

3. After about ten seconds, blindfold a second child and start him/her on the course!

4. Continue like this, until all the other children (who want to) have had a turn.

You will need:
to set this up!
a length of rope
blindfolds

You may need:
a stopwatch
small prizes!

[You can time each child and turn this into a competition, if you wish!]

5. With the whole group together again, ask your children to talk a bit about their experience in this game...

To Tie This in:

Hanging on to the rope was the key to doing well: if you let go, you could wander off and not get round the course! The rope didn't make the obstacles disappear, but it did help you to get round them ~ God might not make the hard things in our lives disappear, but when we pray, He definitely helps us through them!

HELP!

You will need:
to prepare some situations
to brief your co-leaders!
paper
suitable pens

In advance, write each of the situations you thought of for SET THE SCENE (eg being bullied, starting a new school, going to the dentist...) on separate pieces of paper. Give one to each of your co-leaders. Ask them to develop the situation into a bit of a story (eg "There's a bunch of older kids down my road who are giving me a really hard time at the moment. The other night they...." and so on) - ask them not to make it too involved!

1. Have everyone sitting in their small groups **or** ask your children to get into as many groups as you have leaders!

2. Then explain: *'the leader in your group has a problem... listen carefully to what it is, then see if you can think of any ways to help!'*

3. ...Each leader then tells their 'story' to the children in their small group and asks for their advice - they may well need some help with this! Ask your leaders to note down any bits of good advice as they go along.

   [As your children have the chance to think these situations through, they may well be working out some answers to problems they really do face...]

4. Move each group round to a different leader after about five minutes, and repeat point 3 above... Do this again, as appropriate!

5. With the whole group together again, ask each leader to just say briefly what advice they were given, then talk about it together.

To Tie This in:

When Nehemiah hit hard times, he prayed and then he did something about the problem. As Nehemiah found out, God might not make the hard things in our lives disappear, but when we pray, He definitely helps us through them!

WALL-BUILDERS

In advance, get together some junk materials which can be used to make 'building bricks' (eg empty packets and cartons, newspaper - see diagram below for how to make newspapers into 'bricks'!). Guess how many teams you will have, and share the materials out into that many bags - it's important that each team starts off with roughly the same 'building equipment'!

1. Have everyone sitting in their small groups **or** ask your children to get into teams of about six.

2. Give each team a bag of 'building material', sticky tape **and/or** blob of Blu-tack.

3. Explain the game: *'like Nehemiah and the people of Jerusalem, your job is to build a strong wall from the things in your bag. You can use the newspaper to make 'bricks'...*

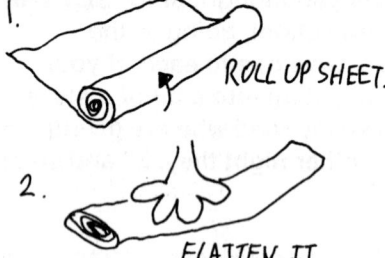
1. ROLL UP SHEET.
2. FLATTEN IT.

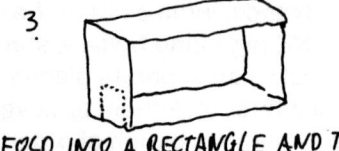
3. FOLD INTO A RECTANGLE AND TAPE AT CORNER.

4. FILL WITH SCRUNCHED UP PAPER.

...and the sticky tape and/or Blu-tack to make the wall secure. Go!'

4. Stop this after about ten minutes...

5. ...Have an opportunity to look together at each team's wall - draw attention to the good points of each one (ie strength, progress made etc) and decide on a winner!

 **To Tie This in:**

This is really just to reinforce the story content! However, you could also draw out the importance of teamwork.

You will need:
to collect together some 'building materials'
carrier bags
sticky tape **and/or** Blu-tack

You may need:
small prizes!

ADDITIONAL IDEAS:

1. Invite someone who is into rock-climbing or mountaineering to come and talk **or** be interviewed about it. Ask them to bring pictures **and/or** some of their equipment to show. Make sure they say how they use rope!

2. With older children, organise a climbing wall (**or** abseiling) session at a local sports or activity centre. Again, highlight the use of rope and link it in with the teaching content, as appropriate.

The Adventures of Nehemiah - Part 2

✱ Draw in here people building the city.
They might be climbing ladders, carrying stones, carving blocks of stone etc.

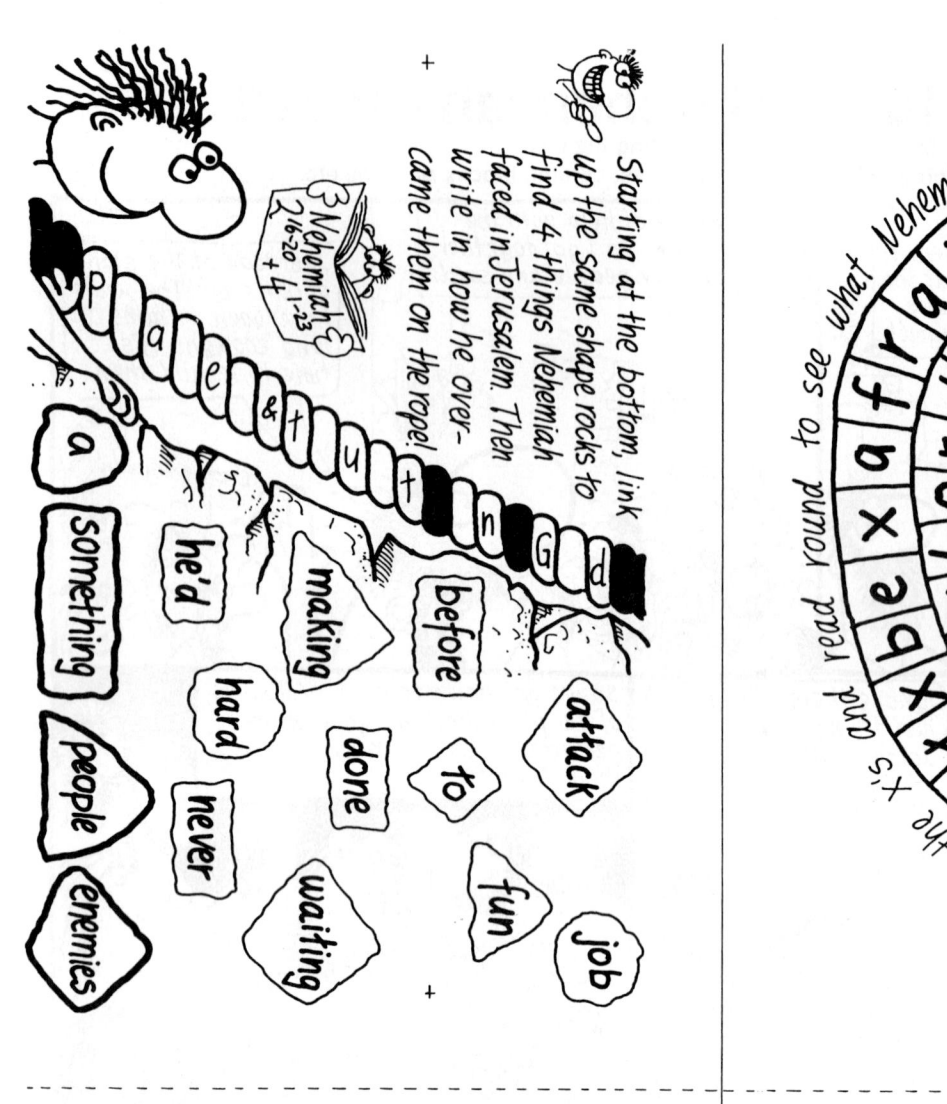

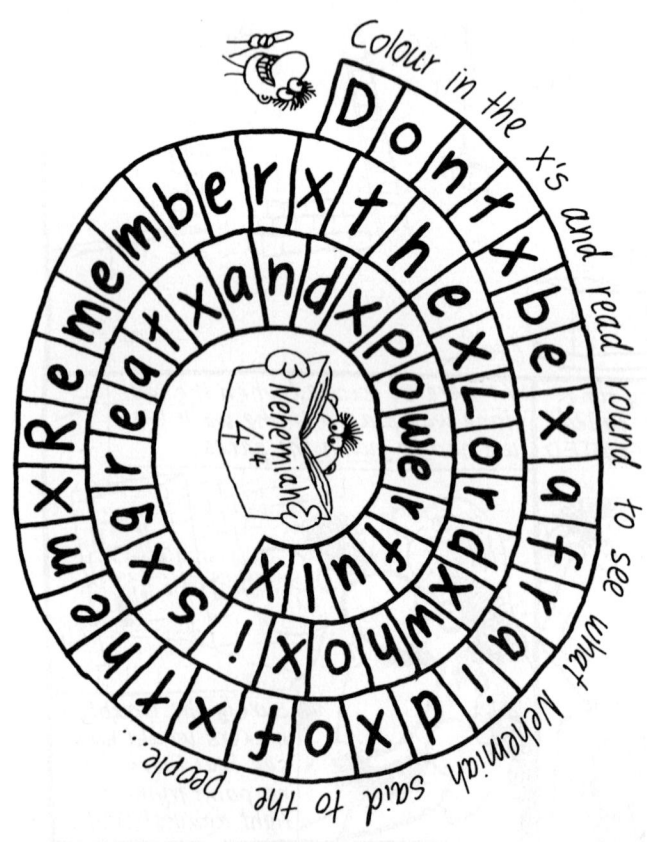

3 Nehemiah

LEADERS OVERVIEW

Out on the water, a yacht looks tiny and insignificant against the power of the wind and the waves... but the experienced sailor is not alarmed: the direction and speed of the boat can be quickly altered by pulling on the ropes (called 'sheets'). And by 'tacking', even an unfavourable wind can be used to make progress.

Only the gates were needed to complete the walls of Jerusalem, but Nehemiah's enemies weren't about to give in: in fact, their attempts to stop him became even more devious and personal. Despite weeks of exhausting effort, Nehemiah did not 'keel' over! He prayed and took avoiding action.

Nehemiah's prayer was simple: 'God, make me strong!'. His closeness to God helped him recognise and deal with the opposition he faced. And God did give him the strength he needed to complete the task.

We all need stamina! God does not always remove our difficulties, but He is with us in them, building character as we persevere. Some of our children face tough, ongoing situations... let's encourage them to pray for the strength God promises!

Nehemiah did not give up despite considerable opposition... PRAY especially for children in your group with specific problems at the moment: that God would give them all they need to keep going and grow through them... PRAY also for any who seem to give up trying very easily.

We Would Like Our Children to...

... see that through prayer God gives us strength.

Key Verse

I prayed, "God, make me strong."
Nehemiah 6:9

Bible Base

Nehemiah 6:1-16
(More Problems for Nehemiah to The Wall is Finished)

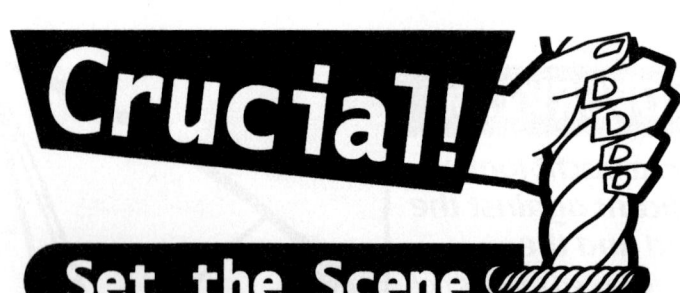

Crucial!

Set the Scene

In advance, organise a short aerobics routine *or* mini-circuit (eg bunny hops, shuttle runs, bench presses...) *or* tests of strength (eg tug of war, arm wrestling...) to get your children to experience the need for physical strength and stamina! If you don't have the space for everyone to be active, then have a 'contestant and audience' version, with volunteers competing against each other.

1. Simply run the aerobics **or** mini-circuit **or** tests of strength.

2. Get some comments and feedback about strength as you go along, eg *do you feel strong enough to do this? Have you got the strength to keep going?* ...and so on.

You will need:
to organise this!

You may need:
music
small prizes!

Present the Bible Base

Option A: Cartoon Strip

In advance, make copies of the cartoon strip version of the Bible story on page 23 - enough for one each.

Simply help your children get to grips with the story! Also, ask them to draw people celebrating in the picture marked *.

You will need:
to make copies
pens **or** pencils

Option B: Dramatic Presentation

In advance, work out a short drama, using the cartoon strip version of the Bible story on page 23 as the script!

Perform the drama! Involve your children by asking them to act out being at the 'celebration party', as suggested in the cartoon strip version.

You will need:
to practise!

Focus...

Either in small groups **or** altogether, ask questions to bring out the main points, such as:

➤ *What did the troublemakers do to try and stop the re-building work this time?*

[Help your children recall that the troublemakers spread lies about Nehemiah, tried to get him on his own and paid someone to scare him! Perhaps also ask your children to talk about a time when someone spread lies about them...]

➤ *Do you think Nehemiah ever felt like giving up? Why/ why not?*

[Help your children think how Nehemiah might have felt about the problems he faced.]

➤ *...But Nehemiah did finish re-building the walls: how come?*

[There are several possible answers, but bring out clearly that Nehemiah was only able to re-build the walls because he had God's help. Nehemiah was no 'superhero'! He was just an ordinary man who talked with an extraordinary God!]

Pray!

You will need:
to make more bricks
to prepare the verse
pens **or** pencils
Blu-tack

In advance, choose <u>how</u> you want to pray from LEARNING TO PRAY on pages vii to x. Make more 'bricks' as described on page 11: use a different coloured paper <u>or</u> card <u>or</u> pen to distinguish them from the 'bricks' you had last session! Also, write out Nehemiah's prayer - 'God, make me strong!' - on a long strip of paper.

1. **Either** in small groups **or** altogether, ask: **when do <u>we</u> need to be strong?** Link back to SET THE SCENE to start them thinking... then go on to talk together about the strength we need in other situations, as appropriate to your children:
   - to face something new or difficult (eg an operation, home situation);
   - to keep trying when we find something tough (eg at school);
   - to be ourselves;
   - to do things God's way;
   - not to give in to doing something wrong ...and so on.

2. Remind your children about Nehemiah's prayers by saying something like: **'Nehemiah's enemies were strong and clever, but Nehemiah knew that God is far stronger and much cleverer! He prayed: 'God, make me strong!'. When we are finding it hard to keep going or feel like giving up, we can talk with God too. He really wants to help...'**

3. **NOW PRAY!** Base your prayer-time on the idea you have chosen from pages vii to x. Use the 'bricks' as appropriate, eg:

   ● add them to your 'prayer wall' from last session. Have the names **and/or** situations mentioned in point 1 above written out on separate 'bricks' and tack them together. Perhaps put Nehemiah's prayer underneath the whole thing as a 'foundation'. (And keep the 'prayer wall' going as outlined on page 11.)

   ● ask your children to write **and/or** draw (**or** dictate) their own prayers on separate 'bricks'. Then pray them! Ask everyone to join in with **'God, make him/her/them strong!'** after each prayer.

Extra Teaching

Quiz

You will need:
to prepare the grid
to make two yacht
  shapes
Blu-tack
a broad, bold pen

You may need:
paper
pens **or** pencils
small prizes!

In advance, draw two large grids on separate (preferably blue) pieces of paper - they should be five squares down and twenty squares across. Also, cut out two yacht shapes (about the same size as one square) from different coloured paper <u>or</u> card. (Diagram over the page.)

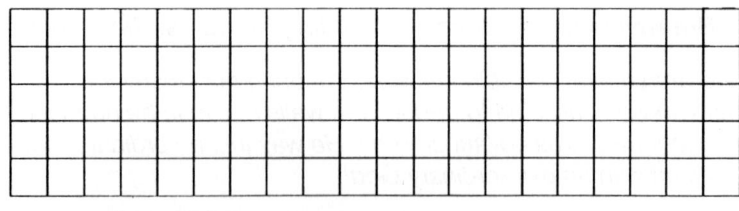
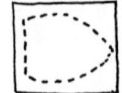 CUT OUT A BOAT SHAPE

1. Ask your children to get into two equal-sized teams.

2. **Either** ask each team to think of six questions about Nehemiah's story to put to the opposing team... **or** get ready to ask the questions on page 25.

3. Give each team a grid and a pen - ask them to put an arrow (←) in any five squares to represent the wind... but no more than two in adjoining squares! This is now the quiz grid for the opposing team.

4. Explain the quiz: *'you can move your yacht each time you get a question right. The yachts move diagonally ('tack'). Your yacht cannot enter a square with an arrow in it. For each correct answer, you can move up to three squares in one direction only. The team whose yacht moves furthest, wins!'*

 START LINE
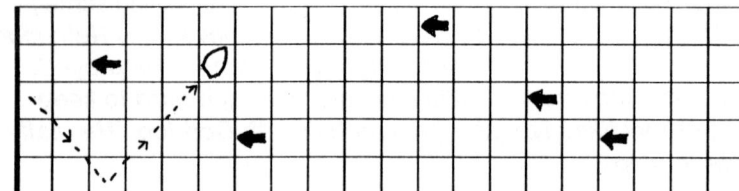

5. Run the quiz, asking the questions to each team in turn.

 **To Tie This in:**

When the wind is blowing against a yacht, a sailor can still zigzag forward ('tack') by using ropes (called 'sheets') ~ when other people were against him, Nehemiah knew that God would help him keep going as he carried on praying! (Knowing what God did for Nehemiah helped your children do well in the quiz ~ knowing what God has done for others can help us keep going when things are against us!)

Prayer Notes

In advance, prepare the 'prayer notes' on page 24 - see page 4 for guidance!

1. Give each child one of the folded 'prayer notes'.

2. Ask your children to complete and colour the picture, and complete the key verse on the other half of the sheet.

3. Also, ask your children to think of *times when we need to be strong...*

You will need:
to prepare the 'prayer notes'
coloured pens **or** pencils

4. ...Ask them to write these things **or** draw pictures of them inside their 'prayer notes'.

5. Finally, ask your children to add this session's 'prayer notes' to the first two by threading the string through the two holes and tying it at the front.

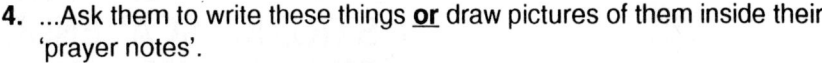

Extra Activities

PIRATES!

You will need:
six spoons
chairs
lots of space!

You may need:
small prizes!

1. Have everyone in their small groups **or** ask your children to get into teams of six.

2. Put the six spoons on one chair in the middle of your meeting room... then place chairs around it - one for each team - some distance away.

3. Have each team line up in height order - the smallest child first! - and give each child a number.

4. Explain the game: *'when I call out your number, run and grab **one** spoon and bring it back to your team's chair. Once the spoons have all gone from the middle, you can take **one** spoon from another team's chair. You can only carry one spoon at a time! Keep going until you have three spoons on your chair at once.'*

   [Watch out for other team members hiding spoons to stop them being taken!]

5. Run the game, giving a point to the child who gets three spoons on the chair at once in each round. The team with the most points, wins!

 **To Tie This in:**

Did your children find it hard to keep going in this game? How did they feel when one of their spoons was taken? Do we give up easily, especially when things seem to be going against us? Nehemiah's story reminds us to ask God to make us strong... and then keep going!

STRING SCAVENGE

In advance, cut <u>many</u> short lengths of string <u>or</u> wool. Scatter them around your meeting room and preferably also around a larger outdoor area.

1. Have everyone in their small groups <u>or</u> ask your children to get into teams of six.

2. Explain the first part of the game: *'you have to run and collect as many pieces of string (<u>or</u> wool) as you can!'*

3. ...Allow plenty of time for this! Notice when children are beginning to flag - then stop and get everybody together again.

4. Explain the second part of the game: *'now tie all your pieces of string (<u>or</u> wool) together!'*

5. Lay out the lengths of string (<u>or</u> wool) side by side to compare them - the team with the longest piece, wins!

To Tie This in:

This is a tiring game: did your children find it hard to keep going? Do we give up easily, especially when things take a long time to finish? Nehemiah's story reminds us to ask God to make us strong... and then keep going right to the end!

You will need:
to set this up

You may need:
small prizes!

SALT DOUGH MODELS

In advance, make the salt dough: simply mix 4oz salt, 8oz plain flour, 2tbsp cooking oil and 4floz water together in a large bowl. Add more water until the dough resembles pastry. Then knead the dough - the more you knead, the easier the dough will be to mould. Wrap the dough in plastic to keep it moist.

1. Simply have your children use the dough to make people, animals, flowers, letters... and so on.

2. After the session, bake the models at 70°C, for about 2 hours - do check thinner models at regular intervals, so that they do not burn!

3. <u>Either</u> varnish the models yourself, <u>or</u> take them to the next session for your children to paint <u>and/or</u> varnish.

ALTERNATIVE IDEA:
Make models from Fimo instead!

To Tie This in:

Who would choose to sit in an oven for an hour?! Nobody, but the salt dough (or Fimo) needs the heat of the oven to become strong ~ we would not choose hard times in our lives, but God does make us stronger as we keep going with him through them.

You will need:
to make the salt dough
varnish
baking tray(s)

You may need:
poster paints
kitchen tools (eg rolling pin, butter knives, pastry shapes, garlic press (good for making hair!)...

The Adventures of Nehemiah - Part 3

✱ Draw in here lots of people singing, dancing, enjoying themselves and praising God!

QUIZ QUESTIONS

Please read these through in advance and adapt them to suit your children if necessary! Some of the questions have more than one answer, so decide what you are going to accept as correct - children have a very strong sense of fairness!

Session 1

Your Answers!

1. What was Nehemiah's job? _____

2. What news did Nehemiah's brother Hanani tell him? _____

3. What did Nehemiah do first? _____

4. What did the king promise Nehemiah? _____

Session 2

1. What did Nehemiah do before starting work on the city walls? _____

2. What did the troublemakers do to try and stop Nehemiah rebuilding the walls? _____

3. What did Nehemiah do about the troublemakers? _____

4. Why did the troublemakers' plans fail? _____

Session 3

1. What new things did the troublemakers try to stop the walls being finished? _____

2. What did Nehemiah ask God to do? _____

3. What did Nehemiah and the people of Jerusalem do when the walls were finished? _____

4. What can we learn about God from Nehemiah's story? _____

QUIZ QUESTIONS

(Please read these through in advance and adapt them to suit your children if necessary. Some of the questions have more than one answer, so decide what you are going to accept as correct. Children have a very strong sense of fairness!)

Session 1

Your Answer:

1. What was Nehemiah's job?

2. What news did Nehemiah's brother Hanani tell him?

3. What did Nehemiah do first?

4. What did the king promise Nehemiah?

Session 2

1. How did Nehemiah organise the work on the city walls?

2. What did the troublemakers do to try and stop Nehemiah rebuilding the walls?

3. What did Nehemiah do about the troublemakers?

4. Why did the troublemakers' plans fail?

Session 3

1. What new things did the troublemakers try to stop the walls being finished?

2. What did Nehemiah ask God to do?

3. What did Nehemiah and the people of Jerusalem do when the walls were finished?

4. What can we learn about God from Nehemiah's story?

26

4 Daniel

LEADERS OVERVIEW

999...! Firefighters are ready to react instantly to any emergency call. They may be experienced and well-equipped, but they never work alone: in a smoke-filled building, firefighters rely on a crucial system of ropes (called 'lines') to guide them and link them to the vital support team outside.

Daniel faced many challenges in his life. He was among those taken prisoner when King Nebuchadnezzar's army invaded Judah in around 600 BC. Once in Babylon, Daniel's qualities were quickly recognised and he was promoted in the king's service - thing's were looking up! But the king was not a reasonable man: when none of the court magicians were able to guess his dream and interpret its meaning, he sentenced all his advisers to death. And that included Daniel and his friends...

Daniel did not panic, but like any trained firefighter, he recognised the part others could play. He asked his would-be executioner for more time and set about getting crucial prayer support!

Let's help our children to understand that they do something really important for other people when they pray for them. Let's encourage them, too, to ask for prayer themselves... Together we will find that God is more than equal to any problem!

Daniel knew where to look for answers... Nebuchadnezzar certainly did not!! PRAY against the subtle influences which will already be telling our children that God is just one of many options: ask God to reveal His true self to them!

We Would Like Our Children to...

... see that (group) prayer is powerful.

Key Verse

Daniel asked his friends to pray...
Daniel 2:18

Bible Base

Daniel 2:1-49
(Nebuchadnezzar's Dream and The Meaning of the Dream)

Crucial!

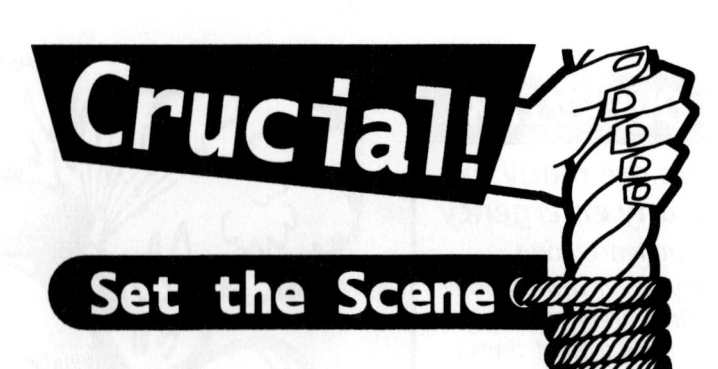

Set the Scene

1. Give everyone a small piece of paper and a pen **or** pencil.

2. Ask everyone to draw anything they like on their piece of paper, keeping it secret from everyone else!

3. Now ask everyone to fold their drawings and write their names on the outside.

4. Tack each drawing onto a board **or** wall, with the names clearly visible.

5. With the whole group together again, ask a child to choose a name and guess what that person drew. (If, by chance, he/she does guess correctly, ask for details about the drawing!) Do this several times!

6. Bring out the obvious point: *'it's impossible to guess (in detail) what someone else has drawn, because we cannot read someone else's mind...'*

You will need:
(thickish) paper
pens **or** pencils
Blu-tack

Present the Bible Base

Option A: Visual!

In advance, decide how you are going to use the pictures on pages 35 to 40 - then prepare them! Possibilities include:

- OHP - photocopy *or* trace each picture onto a separate OHP acetate. Add some colour!

- CARTOON STRIP - simply photocopy each picture and add some colour! You could paste the pictures to a roll of wallpaper, then unroll it bit by bit as you tell the story.

- STORY BOARD - photocopy the pictures, cut out the characters and add some colour! Use Blu-tack *or* magnetic strip *or* velcro to stick the pictures to whatever surface you have available! Move the characters around as you tell the story.

Now tell the story, using the pictures and the paraphrase on page 34 as a basis!

You will need:
to prepare the pictures

Option B: Drama

1. Ask your children to get into groups of between seven and ten.

2. Ask each group to decide who is going to play the following people in the Bible story: **DANIEL, KING NEBUCHADNEZZAR, SHADRACH, MESHACH, ABEDNEGO, ARIOCH** (the commander of the king's guards) ...and ask the rest to play **MAGICIANS** or **ADVISERS**!

3. Now tell the story <u>twice</u>, using the paraphrase on page 34 as a basis. <u>First time round</u>, ask your children to listen out for the person they are going to play... <u>Second time round</u>, encourage them to act out the action as you tell the story!

Focus...

<u>Either</u> in small groups <u>or</u> altogether, ask questions to bring out the main points, such as:

➤ *How was Daniel able to find out what the king's dream was?*

[There are several possible answers, but highlight how important it was that his three friends prayed.]

➤ *Why do you think that the prayers of Daniel's three friends made such a difference?*

[Bring out the idea that prayer asks God to get involved... and He can do everything! If appropriate, also read what Jesus said about praying together in Matthew 18:19-20.*]*

Pray!

You will need:
to think of a person or situation
some things to show...
a board <u>or</u> large sheet of paper
suitable pens

You may need:
several balls of string <u>or</u> wool

In advance, choose <u>how</u> you want to pray from LEARNING TO PRAY on pages vii to x. Also, think of a person <u>or</u> people in some kind of need (eg someone from your group who has just moved away from the area; a situation in the news...). Make sure that you choose someone who will interest your children, otherwise they may not care enough to pray! Also, get together some things about that person to show (eg a photo, a letter, a news headline...).

1. Show the photo (<u>or</u> whatever you have) and talk together <u>very briefly</u> about the person <u>or</u> people you have chosen.

2. Ask: *what do you think he/she/they might need at the moment?* (eg the child who has moved away might need to make new friends... and so on).

3. Ask: *what can we do to help <u>right now</u>?* Someone will hopefully say 'pray!', but remind your children about the story if they need a hint!

4. Then ask: *who else needs help right now?* Try to encourage your children to think of people and situations further afield than those they have prayed about so far in this series - note these names on the board <u>or</u> paper as you go along.

5. Remind your children about Daniel's friends' prayers by saying something like: *'Daniel really needed help and he knew straightaway what was the best thing to do: getting his friends to pray was more powerful than arguing, fighting, thinking, planning, panicking(!), because praying gets God involved...! Just like Daniel's friends, our prayers for other people really can make a difference...'*

6. **NOW PRAY!** Base your prayer-time on the idea you have chosen from pages vii to x. Use the string <u>or</u> wool as appropriate, eg:

   ● ask your children to get into friendship groups. Ask each group to form a circle. Give one person in each group a ball of string <u>or</u> wool. Ask him/her to pray for <u>one</u> of the people on your list. Then have him/her hold the end of the string, but pass the ball to someone else - he/she prays for another person on your list, then holds on to the string, but passes the ball on ...and so on. Perhaps make a few comments at the end about group prayer, using the string 'webs' as an illustration!

7. Perhaps finish by saying something like: **'I wonder if there is anyone here who would like someone to pray for them, like Daniel's three friends did for him...'** As appropriate, pray for them there and then **or** say when you will be available to listen and pray.

[Please check the guidelines on praying alone with a child on page vii.]

Extra Teaching

Key Verse

In advance, write the key verse on page 27 onto a large piece of paper (or choose another verse, eg *Matthew 18:19-20*). Guess how many children will be at your session, and cut the verse into that many pieces! Also, think of a suitable forfeit <u>for the whole group</u>. Write out the forfeit, starting: 'everybody in the room has to....' and put it in a sealed envelope, marked FORFEIT!

1. Ask for a volunteer... choose someone who is well-liked by the rest of the group, and ask him/her to come to the front.

2. Ask another leader **or** child to spread the pieces of the key verse out around your meeting room (but <u>not</u> on the floor), while you explain the game: **'you (the volunteer) have <u>two minutes</u> to piece together a verse from the Bible about prayer. However, you are <u>not</u> allowed to move from where you are standing now...** Let this sink in, then add: **...and if you (the volunteer) cannot get the verse together, there will be a forfeit!**

3. Just wait and see what happens next! The volunteer might attempt to get the pieces **or** he/she might ask for help **or** some children might offer to fetch the pieces for him/her... let the group decide what is going to happen, and run the challenge!

4. Stop the action after two minutes...

    ... **if the verse has <u>not</u> been pieced together,** ask the volunteer to open the envelope to reveal that the forfeit is for everyone! And do the forfeit!

    ... **if the verse <u>has</u> been pieced together,** still ask the volunteer to open the envelope, and point out that the children who helped have saved everyone from a forfeit!

You will need:
to prepare the verse
a forfeit!
a stopwatch
Blu-tack

30

To Tie This in:

When Daniel and his friends chose to help, everyone was saved ~ choosing to help the volunteer saved (or would have saved!) everyone from a forfeit! When we help others in real life, we often find that we are helped too (add detail to this, as appropriate).

Prayer Notes

In advance, prepare the 'prayer notes' on page 41 - see page 4 for guidance!

You will need:
to prepare the
 'prayer notes'
coloured pens **or**
 pencils

Answers:
Rope B links the firefighter and team; Daniel relied on **God** & his **friends**

1. Give each child one of the folded 'prayer notes'.

2. Ask your children to do the puzzle, colour the picture and complete the key verse on the other half of the sheet.

3. Also, ask your children to think of **someone who they would like to pray for:** as above, try to encourage them to think of people and situations further afield than those they have prayed about so far...

4. ...Ask them to write the person's name and situation **or** draw them inside their 'prayer notes'.

5. Finally, ask your children to add this session's 'prayer notes' to the rest by threading the string through the two holes and tying it at the front.

Extra Activities

SOS GAME

You will need:
For each team:
to set up an obstacle course
a torch **or** bicycle lamp
some bright material
 or a flag
a home-made
 megaphone (ie rolled
 up newspaper)
a plastic tub
a teaspoon
a length of rope
 labelled PRAYER

You may need:
prizes!

In advance, set up identical obstacle courses using chairs, clothes which have to be put on... and so on. Put everything else at the end of each obstacle course.

1. Ask your children to get into teams of four or five, preferably with one leader **or** helper per team.

2. Position each team at the start of an obstacle course, and its leader 'on dry land' as far away from the end as possible!

3. Explain the game: *'you are on a ship which is beginning to sink! Your leader is able to rescue you, but you need to let him/her know that you need rescuing! So, one person from each team is going to go over the obstacle course, choose one of the pieces of equipment and take it back to your team. You can then use it to try and contact your leader. If he/she gets the message, he/she will come and carry you back to 'dry land'... but if he/she does not, then send another person to fetch a different piece of equipment and try again!*

cont'd.....

4. ...Secretly tell the leaders that they can only rescue their team when a team member chooses the 'prayer rope'!

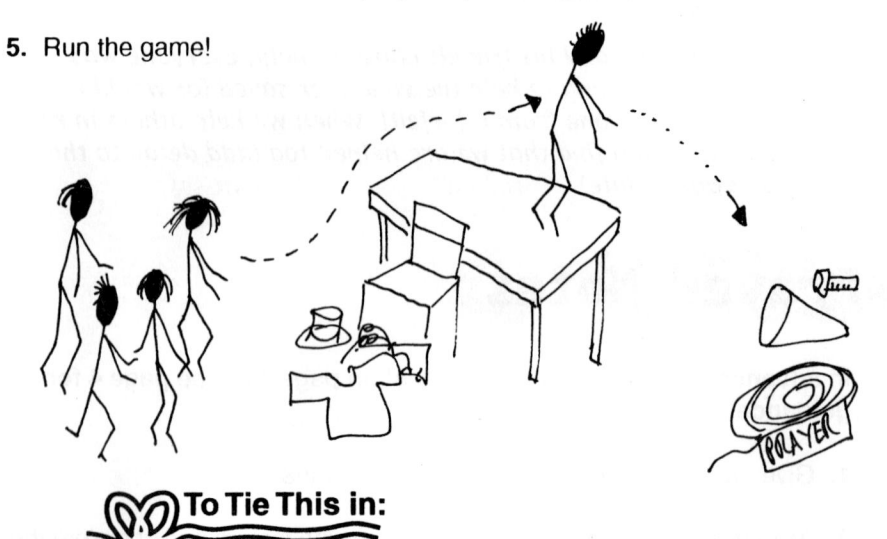

5. Run the game!

To Tie This in:

When did the teams pick up the 'prayer rope' - first, or as a last resort? The first thing Daniel did was to get his friends to pray... prayer is too important to be a last resort!

LOOKING OUT FOR EACH OTHER...

In advance, choose any activity which involves co-operation within a group _or_ team. Possibilities include:

- any team game (eg basketball, unihoc, football, rounders...);
- a large craft project (eg a frieze);
- a quiz _or_ treasure hunt.

Get the appropriate equipment _and/or_ materials together!

1. Ask your children to get into groups **or** teams, as appropriate.

2. Simply run the activity! Watch out for specific instances of children working together...

3. ...Afterwards, talk about helping each other out, using examples from this activity to highlight how important it is!

You will need: to prepare this!

To Tie This in:

Did your children work together in this activity? Daniel's friends were ready to help... and their prayers were crucial! It isn't easy to help others (we're selfish!), but when someone else is in trouble we should be ready to pray and care for them!

'MIND-READING' TRICK

You will need:
to rehearse this well!
a pack of cards

In advance, practise the following code with a co-leader, so that he/she will be able to communicate what is on the card to you!

Signal	Meaning	Aid to Memory
legs crossed	red suit	(red cross)
legs uncrossed	black suit	
blink	clubs/diamonds	(start of alphabet)
yawn	spades/hearts	(end of alphabet)
arms behind back	jack	(back - jack)
arms in lap	queen	(serene queen!)
arms folded	king	(angry king)
head held in hands - number of fingers showing!	1 to 10	

1. Position your co-leader at the back so that he/she can subtly signal to you without your children noticing...!

2. Ask one child to choose a card and show it to everyone else - except you!

3. Say that you are going to try to read your children's minds to find out what the card is...

4. ...Announce what your co-leader signals to you, eg "I can see a picture card... ah yes, it's a king!" ...and so on.

5. Do this three or four more times... see if your children guess the trick!

To Tie This in:

You had to resort to a trick because nobody can read another person's mind! Daniel knew that he could not guess the king's dream... but God could!

ADDITIONAL IDEA:

Invite someone from the fire service to talk about their work. Make sure they mention how they use ropes (called 'lines') and bring out clearly their reliance on a support team.

33

DANIEL 2:1-49
- A PARAPHRASE...

Have you ever needed someone's help? Then you'll know how Daniel felt! Soldiers from another country had invaded his land and taken many people - including Daniel - away. Then he and his three friends were chosen to serve in King Nebuchadnezzar's palace. Daniel felt sad and lonely sometimes, but he knew that God would always be there to help...

1 Very early one morning, the king called all his magicians and advisers together. They could see straight away that he was in a filthy temper.

"Uh oh," one whispered to another, "looks like he got out of the wrong side of the bed this morning..."

"I have had a dream," roared King Nebuchadnezzar, his face purple with rage, "and I want <u>you</u> to tell me what it means! Don't come back until you have the answer! And, if you cannot tell me what my dream means, I'll have you all torn apart and your houses smashed to pieces! Dismissed!"

The magicians and advisers looked at each other - and gulped.

"Er, excuse me, your majesty," said one, "but aren't you just forgetting one small thing? I mean, if you would just be kind enough to tell us what your dream was, I'm sure we could..."

"NO!!" roared King Nebuchadnezzar, "that would be far too easy! Now GO AWAY and get thinking!"

2 The magicians and advisers hurried away. They looked at the stars, checked all sorts of charts and books, and mixed pots of stinky potions... but, of course, none of these things gave them any idea at all about the king's dream! King Nebuchadnezzar was absolutely furious! He ordered that every adviser in the whole country should be killed - and that included Daniel and his three friends. Arioch, the commander of the king's guards, began to sharpen his knife and sent some soldiers to round them all up....

3

4 When Daniel heard the news, he knew he had to act fast... but he did not panic! He went first to see Arioch and heard all about King Nebuchadnezzar's dream. Next, he went to the palace and asked for more time. Then he went to see his three friends - Shadrach, Meshach and Abednego - to ask for their help...

● *What do you think he asked them to do to help him?*

No! What he asked them to do was much more powerful than that... he asked them to PRAY!! So Shadrach, Meshach and Abednego prayed and Daniel went to his room and waited... Suddenly, there it was, in his mind - King Nebuchadnezzar's dream was as clear as if it was his own dream!! Daniel thanked God, then ran to find Arioch: "Don't touch anyone," he puffed, "and take me to see the king!"

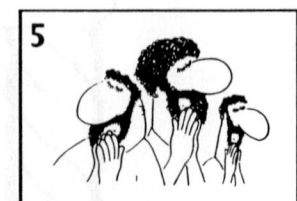

5

6 King Nebuchadnezzar was still fuming!

"Well?" he growled, impatiently, "Can you tell me what I dreamt and what it means?"

Daniel answered, "No magician or adviser can do what you have asked. But there is a God in heaven who explains secret things..." And he went on to tell the king **exactly** what the dream was and what it meant. For several minutes, King Nebuchadnezzar just sat there, staring at Daniel in amazement. And then he said:

"Daniel, now I know that your God is the greatest!"

Daniel 2 - Picture 1

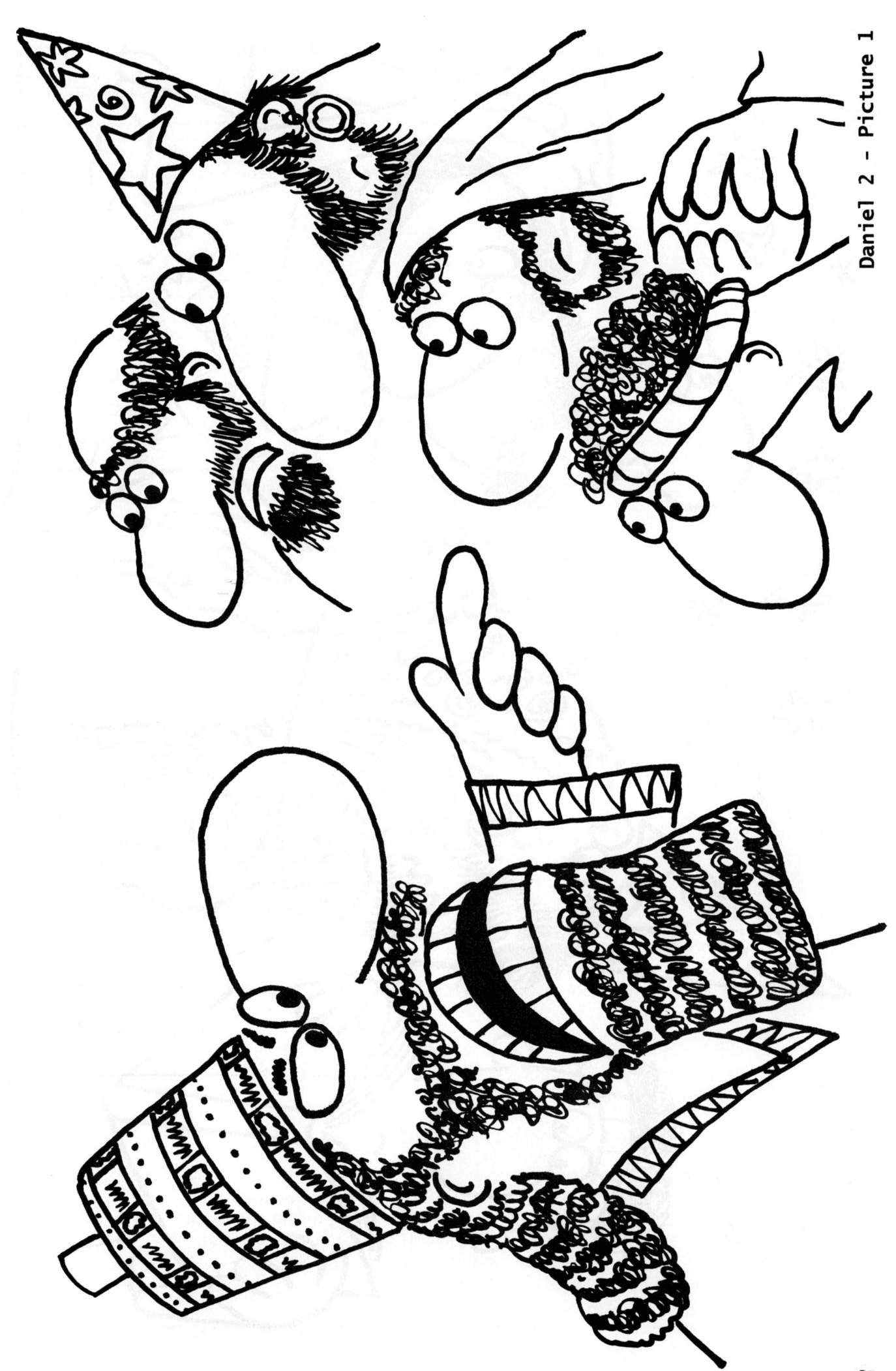

Daniel 2 - Picture 2

Daniel 2 - Picture 3

Daniel 2 - Picture 4

Daniel 2 - Picture 5

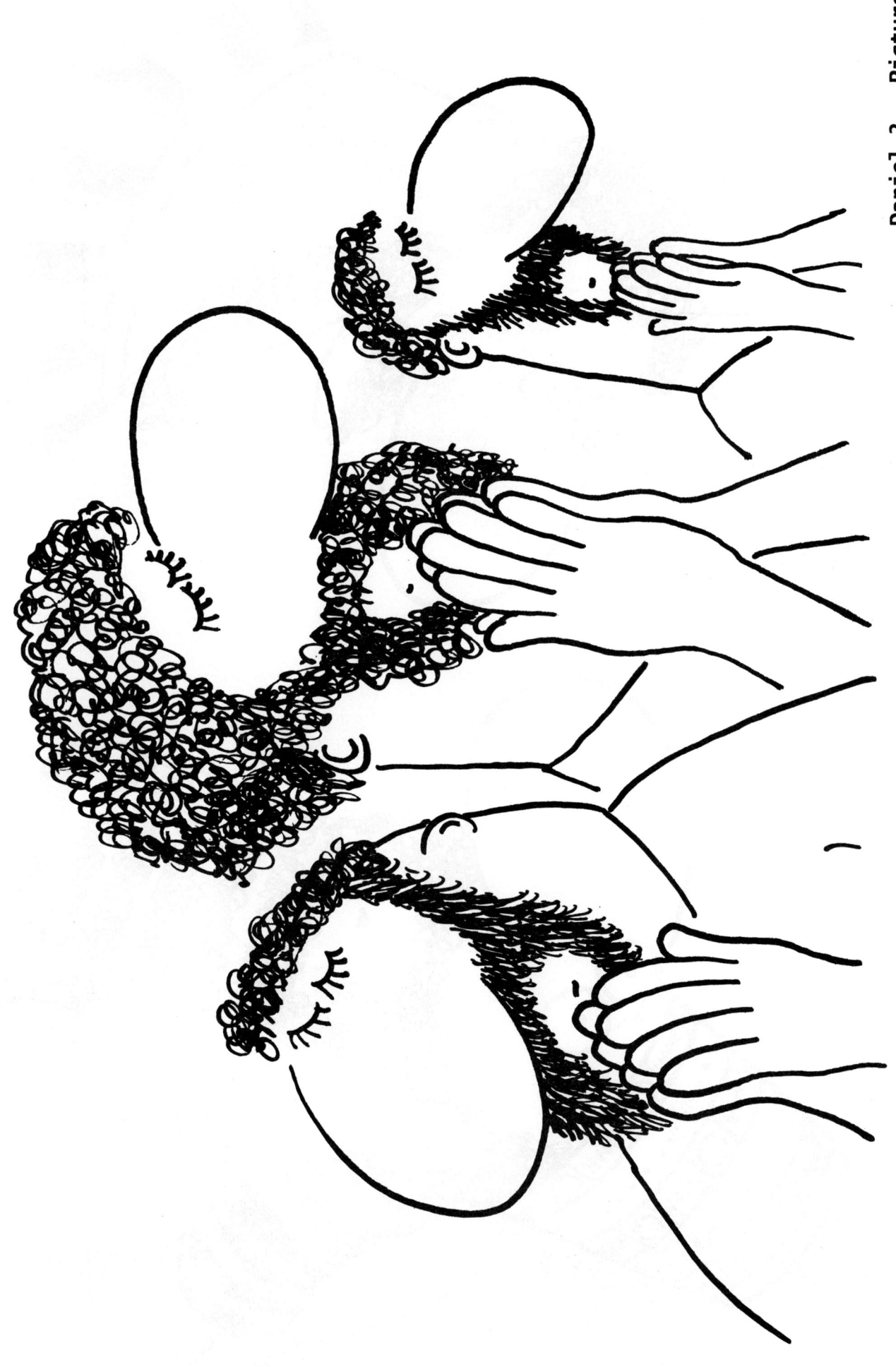

Daniel 2 - Picture 6

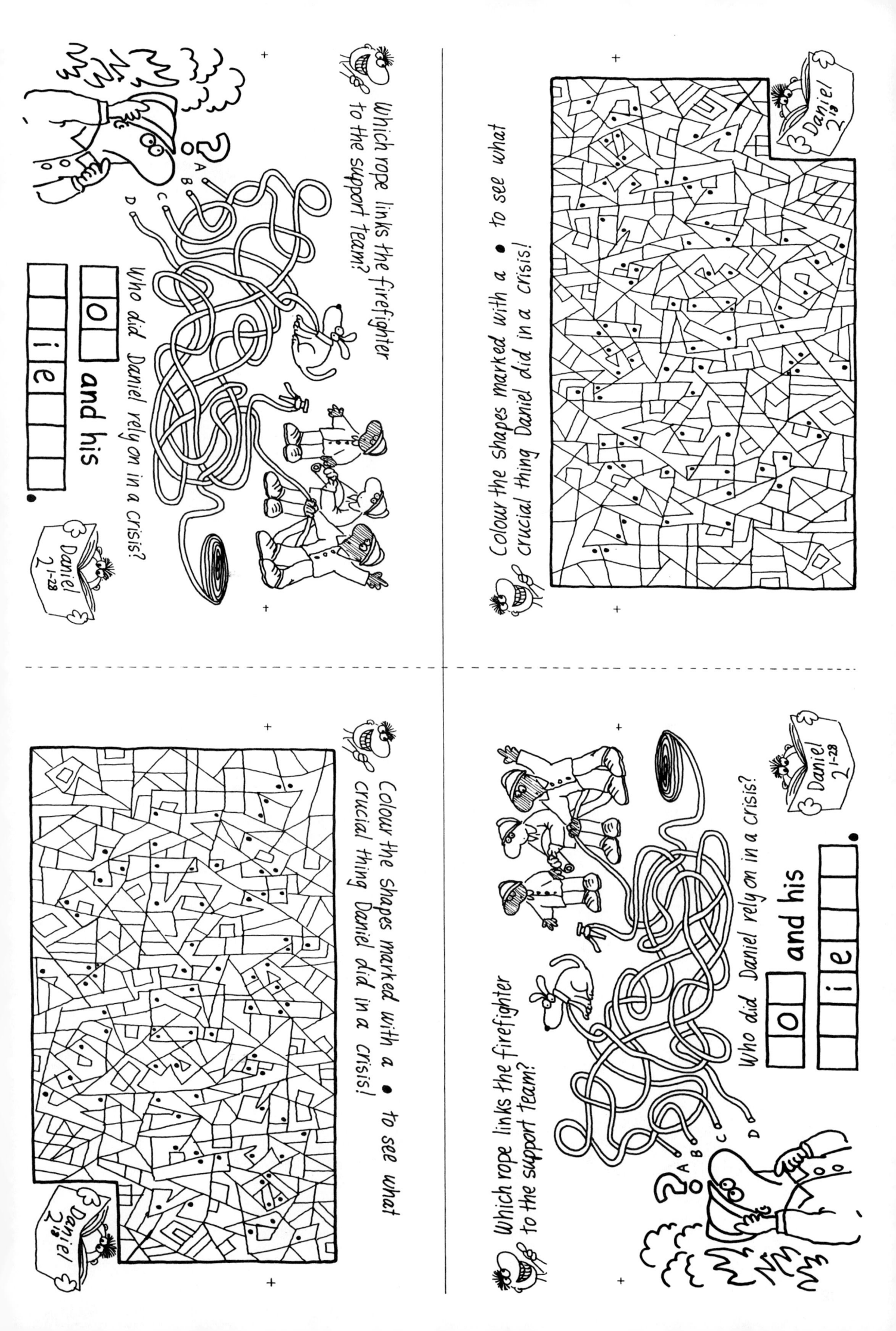

Which rope links the firefighter to the support team?

Who did Daniel rely on in a crisis?

[G] o [d] and his [f] i e [n d s].

Daniel 2:1-28

Colour the shapes marked with a ● to see what crucial thing Daniel did in a crisis!

Daniel 2:18

Colour the shapes marked with a ● to see what crucial thing Daniel did in a crisis!

Daniel 2:18

Which rope links the firefighter to the support team?

Who did Daniel rely on in a crisis?

[G] o [d] and his [f] i e [n d s].

Daniel 2:1-28

5 Daniel

LEADERS OVERVIEW

Strings of bunting, colour, noise, excitement... everyone enjoys a carnival atmosphere!

King Nebuchadnezzar planned an amazing carnival with his own statue as the centre-piece! But he had not planned on the rebellion of Shadrach, Meshach and Abednego, who absolutely refused to bow down and worship any 'god' but their own. In his anger, Nebuchadnezzar had them thrown into a blazing furnace. What happened next made him command everyone in his vast empire to join together in praise and celebration of the one true God!

For many people, prayer is just asking God for things... we need to help our children understand that praise, worship and thanksgiving are a vital part of prayer. Let's encourage them to channel their natural love of celebration towards praise of our great God!

It would have been easy for Shadrach, Meshach and Abednego to go along with the crowd... and our children also face pressure to do (or not to do) what everybody else seems to be doing. Ask God to give them the courage to stand up for what they know to be right! PRAY that the pressure to conform will not stop them making their own decisions about God.

We Would Like Our Children to...

... see that recognising who God is and thanking Him for all He has done are crucial - and very enjoyable! - parts of prayer!

Key Verse

Daniel said: "Praise God for ever and ever..."
Daniel 2:20

Bible Base

Daniel 3:1-30
(The Golden Idol and Blazing Furnace)

Crucial!

Set the Scene

In advance, think of about eight situations in which we celebrate (eg birthdays, Christmas, weddings, passing a driving test...) Write each situation on a separate piece of paper **or** card.

1. Explain the game: *'you are going to see some mimes (that's acting without speaking) - try and guess what the person in each mime is celebrating!'*

2. Ask a co-leader **or** child to pick one of the cards.

3. Ask him/her to mime the situation... and to keep miming until someone guesses the situation correctly!

4. Do the same with the other situations.

5. If you have time, then ask your children to get into small groups with a leader and talk together about things they have celebrated recently!

You will need:
to prepare some situation 'cards'

Present the Bible Base

Option A: Visual!

In advance, decide how you are going to use the pictures on pages 50 to 55 - then prepare them! See page 28 for suggestions!

Now tell the story, using the pictures and the paraphrase on page 49 as a basis!

You will need:
to prepare the pictures

Option B: Paper Puppet Theatre

1. Have your children get into pairs **or** small groups.

2. Now have

   - one pair **or** small group make a 'gold statue';
   - one pair **or** small group make a flaming furnace -

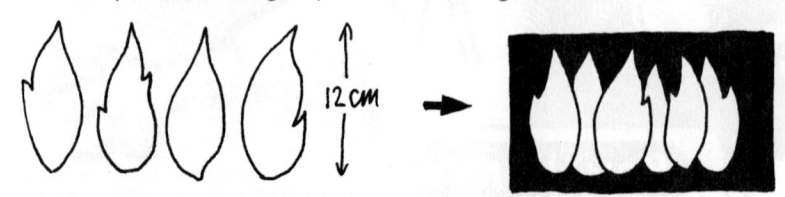

   CUT FLAMES OUT OF COLOURED CARD.
   STICK TO DARK CARD USING BLU-TACK

   [You will need these paper 'flames' for the PRAYER TIME]

   - everyone else make paper bag puppets for **SHADRACH, MESHACH, ABEDNEGO, KING NEBUCHADNEZZAR, CELEBRATION GUESTS** and the **GUARDS**

You will need:
many paper bags!
scrap materials
coloured pens **and/or**
  paints
glue
orange, red and yellow
  coloured paper
dark coloured card
Blu-tack

ADD FACE   ADD HAIR ETC.

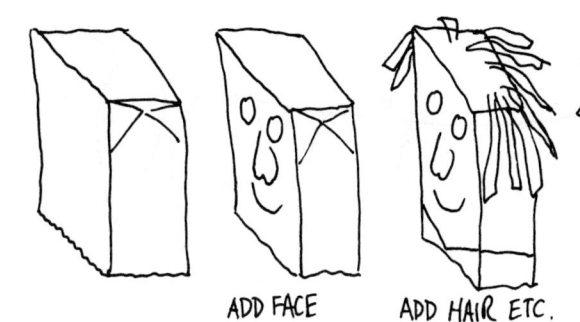

3. Now tell the story <u>twice</u>, using the paraphrase on page 49 as a basis. <u>First time round</u>, ask your children to listen out for the person **or** thing they have made... <u>Second time round</u>, have the puppets 'perform' as you tell the story!

Focus...

<u>Either</u> in small groups **or** altogether, ask questions to bring out the main points, such as:

➤ *Why do you think Shadrach, Meshach and Abednego refused to bow down to King Nebuchadnezzar's gold statue (even though they knew they would be thrown into the flaming furnace...!)?*

[Highlight the idea that there is only one true God... and He is not a statue! As appropriate to your children, help them grasp something of our need to respect God.]

➤ *How do you think Shadrach, Meshach and Abednego felt about God when He rescued them from the flaming furnace?*

[As appropriate, use your children's answers to help them understand what worship is, eg 'when we tell God that He is great, powerful, kind - like Shadrach, Meshach and Abednego did - it's called worship.']

Pray!

You will need:
a flaming furnace!
suitable pens
sellotape **or** a stapler
string

In advance, choose <u>how</u> you want to pray from LEARNING TO PRAY on pages vii to x. Also, if you have not used Option B to help you tell the story, you will need to make 'a flaming furnace': please see point 2 on page 44 for guidance! Have it on display from the outset! Also, cut plenty of spare paper 'flames'.

1. Talk together about things to thank and worship God for.

   [Most children will be aware of things to be thankful for... however, worship will be difficult for those who have as yet made no steps towards God, so don't force it - saying 'thank you' is a good place to start.]

2. Take off the paper flames and give one to each child. Also, give everyone a pen.

3. Now ask your children to get into small friendship groups.

4. Ask everyone to write **or** draw one thing to thank **or** worship God for on each 'flame'...

5. ...Stick **or** staple the 'flames' to the string to make bunting!

cont'd.....

STRING

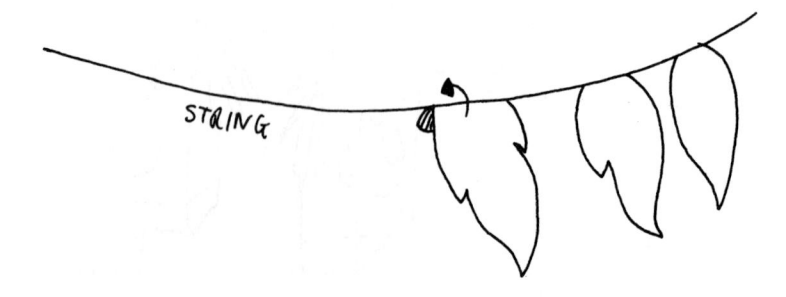

6. NOW PRAY! Base your prayer-time on the idea you have chosen from pages vii to x. Use the bunting as appropriate, eg:

- read each 'flame' in turn and ask your children to join in with 'Thank you, God!' **or** 'Wow, Lord!' after each line, eg

YOU:	Thank You, God, for our families -
EVERYONE:	*Thank You, God!*
YOU:	Thank You, God, for the food we eat -
EVERYONE:	*Thank You, God!*
YOU:	Lord, You are great and powerful -
EVERYONE:	*Wow, Lord!*
YOU:	Lord, You rule over the whole earth -
EVERYONE:	*Wow, Lord!*

  ...and so on.

- encourage individuals to say short 'worship' prayers out loud!

Extra Teaching

Prayer Notes

In advance, prepare the 'prayer notes' on page 56 - see page 4 for guidance!

1. Give each child one of the folded 'prayer notes'.

2. Ask your children to spot the mistakes, colour the picture and complete the key verse on the other half of the sheet.

3. Also, ask your children to think of **things to worship and/or thank God for...**

   [Be ready with ideas!]

4. ...Ask them to write **or** draw these things inside their 'prayer notes'.

5. Finally, ask your children to add this session's 'prayer notes' to the rest by threading the string through the two holes and tying it at the front.

You will need:
to prepare the 'prayer notes'
coloured pens **or** pencils

Answers:
There are 9 obvious mistakes in the picture... the 10th (and biggest) mistake is that they are worshipping the statue!

Worship Time

...How you do this will obviously depend very much on where your children are with God! Worship should engage everyone present in honouring God, so make sure that your children can be part of whatever you plan - it's far better to 'start small' and take everyone with you than to do something which is way beyond the experience and interest of your children at the moment!!

Possibilities include:

- playing a worship song for your children to listen to - either 'live' **or** a taped/CD version;

- learning and joining in with appropriate songs - use a backing track if you do not have any musicians!

- making up actions **or** short dance sequences ...and so on.

Extra Activities

BANNERS

You will need:
garden canes **or** lengths of dowelling
paper **or** cloth
pens **or** paints **or** fabric pens **or** scraps of material
strong tape

1. Perhaps begin by talking together about where your children have seen people using banners and flags (eg at football matches).

2. **Either** altogether **or** in smaller groups, have your children design a banner which says something about God **or** depicts things to thank Him for... If this is beyond the spiritual interest of your children, perhaps have them design a banner to represent your group!

   [Be ready with ideas!]

3. Help your children realise these designs by drawing them on paper **or** painting them **and/or** making a collage on cloth.

4. Secure the designs to canes down one **or** both sides to make the banner(s).

   FOLD OVER AND TAPE

[You could use these banners in the WORSHIP TIME above!]

STATUES QUIZ

In advance, prepare about eight visual questions on well-known statues (eg Nelson's Column, the Statue of Liberty). Perhaps trace *or* copy pictures of statues and ask where *and/or* who they are! Give three answers to choose from for each question so that, even if children have no idea, they can at least have a guess! You could do these visual questions on OHP acetates *or* on separate pieces of paper to be tacked around the walls.

Simply run the quiz in teams **or** friendship groups, as appropriate!

To Tie This in:

Have your children seen any of these statues? If so, what did they do when they saw it? Did they bow down in front of it and tell it how great they thought it was!?! Why not?!! King Nebuchadnezzar made a stupid mistake when he ordered people to bow down and worship his statue... only God deserves our worship - and He isn't a statue!

You will need:
to prepare the questions
paper
pens **or** pencils

You may need:
prizes!

MUSICAL STATUES - WITH A DIFFERENCE!

1. Ask everyone to spread out round the room.

2. Designate a corner - guarded by a leader! - to be the 'flaming furnace'!

3. Explain the game: **'statues wear blue!* You are all going to move round the room whilst the music is playing: When the music stops, be a statue if you are wearing blue... and everybody else get right down on your knees! Anyone who is a statue when they should not be or who moves when there is no music, has to go into the 'flaming furnace' for the next round!'**

   [* Announce something different every round as appropriate to your children, eg 'statues have birthdays in April', 'statues support Manchester United' ...and so on!]

4. Run the game!

To Tie This in:

It would be silly to really worship these other people! God is the greatest. No-one measures up to Him - not even (names of current heroes). Can your children make time to enjoy His company this week - and remember to give Him the respect He deserves?!

You will need:
music
plenty of space!

DANIEL 3:1-30
- A PARAPHRASE...

There was great excitement as the crowds gathered for King Nebuchadnezzar's special carnival celebration.

"What are we here to celebrate?" whispered a guest.

"Search me," whispered another, "perhaps it has to do with that thing over there" - at the front of the crowd was a huge, cloth-covered shape... .

The king's spokesperson stood up, cleared his throat and said: "His supreme and most wonderful excellency has made this new command: whenever you hear the sound of music, you will bow down and worship this, -" and he pointed to the huge shape. Some servants pulled away the cloth.... and everybody gasped: it was a statue made of pure gold!

"Well, it's pretty impressive," whispered the guest, "but if King Nebuchadnezzar thinks I'm going to get down on my knees and tell a statue how great it is, he's got another think coming!"

"Anyone who does not bow down and worship the statue", the spokesperson went on, "will be thrown into the flaming furnace!"

Then the music played, and everybody - including that guest - fell to their knees and began to worship the statue!

From then on, whenever the music played, everybody in the whole country stopped, bowed down and worshipped the statue. Everybody that is, except Daniel's friends - Shadrach, Meschach and Abednego... after all, they knew the one and only true God, and they weren't about to insult Him by bowing down to a statue...

News of this got back to King Nebuchadnezzar. He had Shadrach, Meshach and Abednego appear before him.

"I have heard that you do not serve my gods and you do not bow down to my gold statue," roared King Nebuchadnezzar.

"Now, you know how kind and generous I am," he snarled, "so I am going to give you one last chance. If you bow down and worship my gold statue now, you will go free.... but if you do not, you will be thrown into the flaming furnace!"

"Your majesty", said Shadrach, "we know and worship the one and only God - we would not insult Him by bowing down to anything else! He is able to save us from your flaming furnace! But, even if He chooses not to save us, know this: we will never serve your gods or bow down to your gold statue!"

King Nebuchadnezzar's face went purple with rage....

"What?!" he shouted, "You are willing to die rather than worship my gold statue? Take them to the flaming furnace!" he ordered, "And wait for me - I'm going to enjoy this..."

Nobody could get near the flaming furnace: the heat was so intense and the flames were so bright. Shadrach, Meschach and Abednego were tied up and pushed inside.

"...Er, your most excellent majesty", stuttered one of the king's guards, "Look! They're walking around inside the flaming furnace!"

"In that heat?" said King Nebuchadnezzar, "Don't be ridiculous!" But as he peered into the flames, he did see men walking around. And the strange thing was that there were no longer three men, but four... and the fourth man looked like - well, not like a man - but like an angel...

"Shadrach! Meschach! Abednego!" shouted King Nebuchadnezzar above the roar of the fire, "Come out! Your God has even saved you from the flaming furnace! Now I am sure that He is the greatest! My new command is this: everyone must respect your God. This really is something to celebrate...!"

Daniel 3 - Picture 1

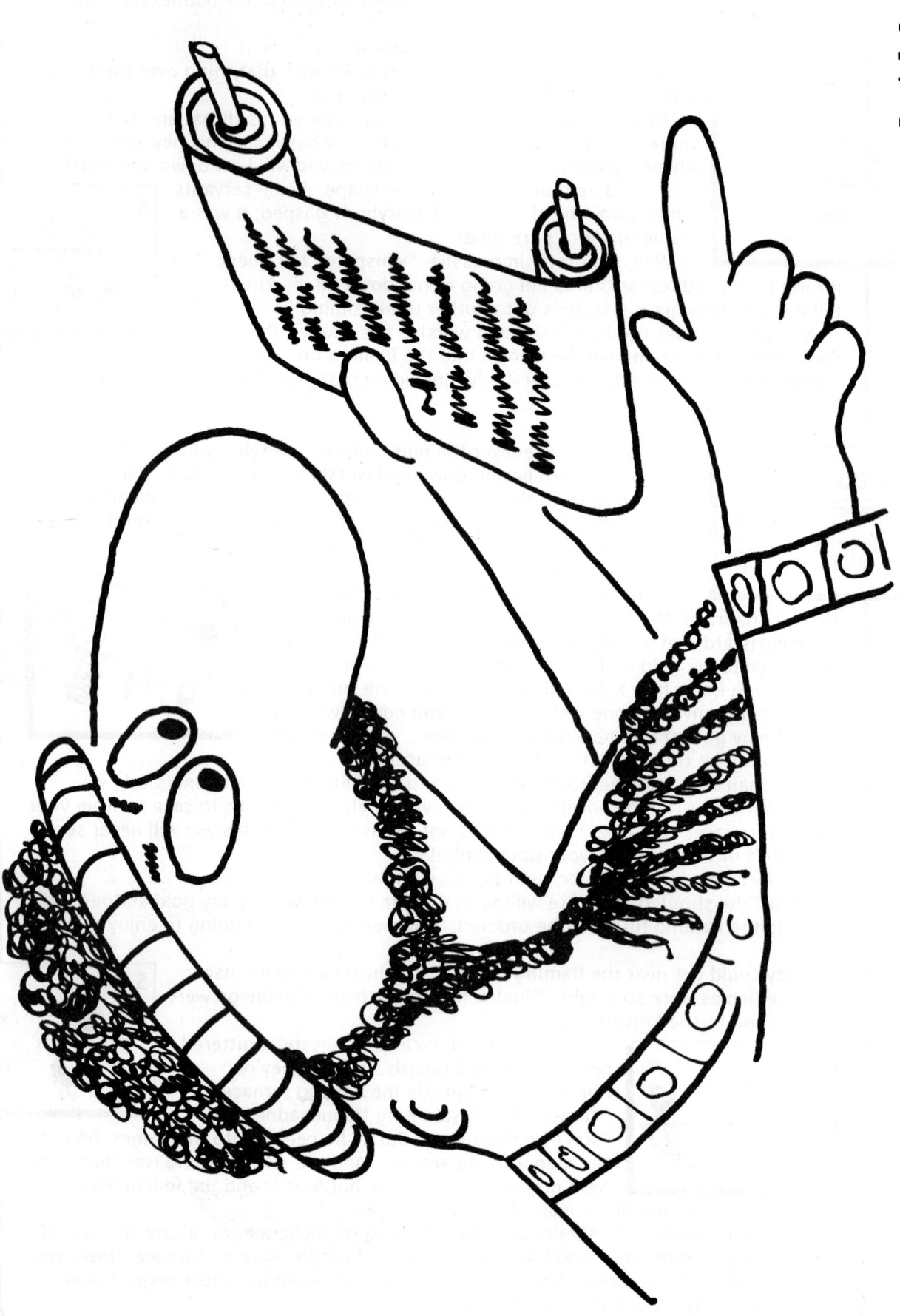

Daniel 3 - Picture 2

Daniel 3 - Picture 3

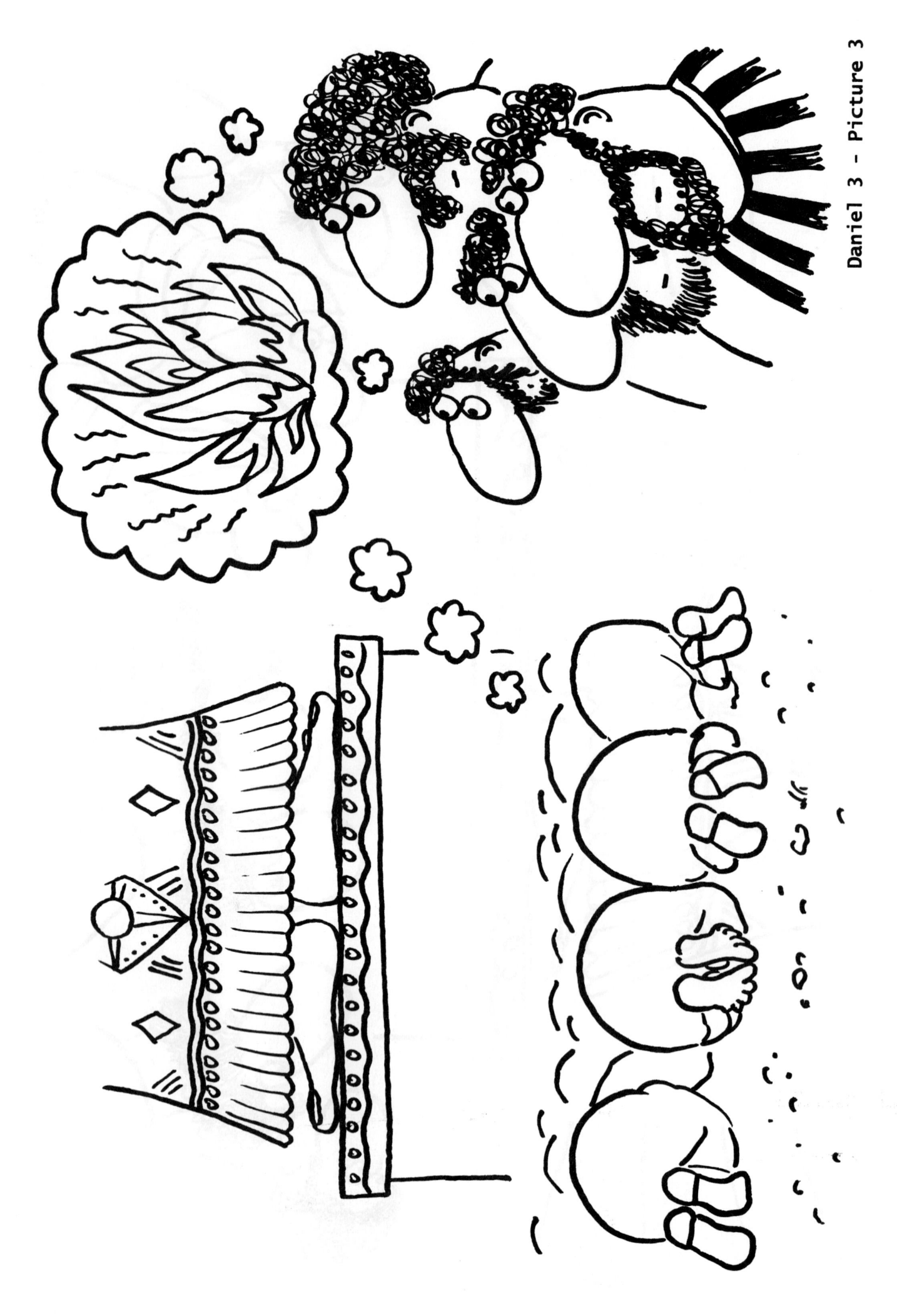

Daniel 3 - Picture 4

Daniel 3 - Picture 5

Daniel 3 - Picture 6

This picture has ten mistakes. Can you spot them?

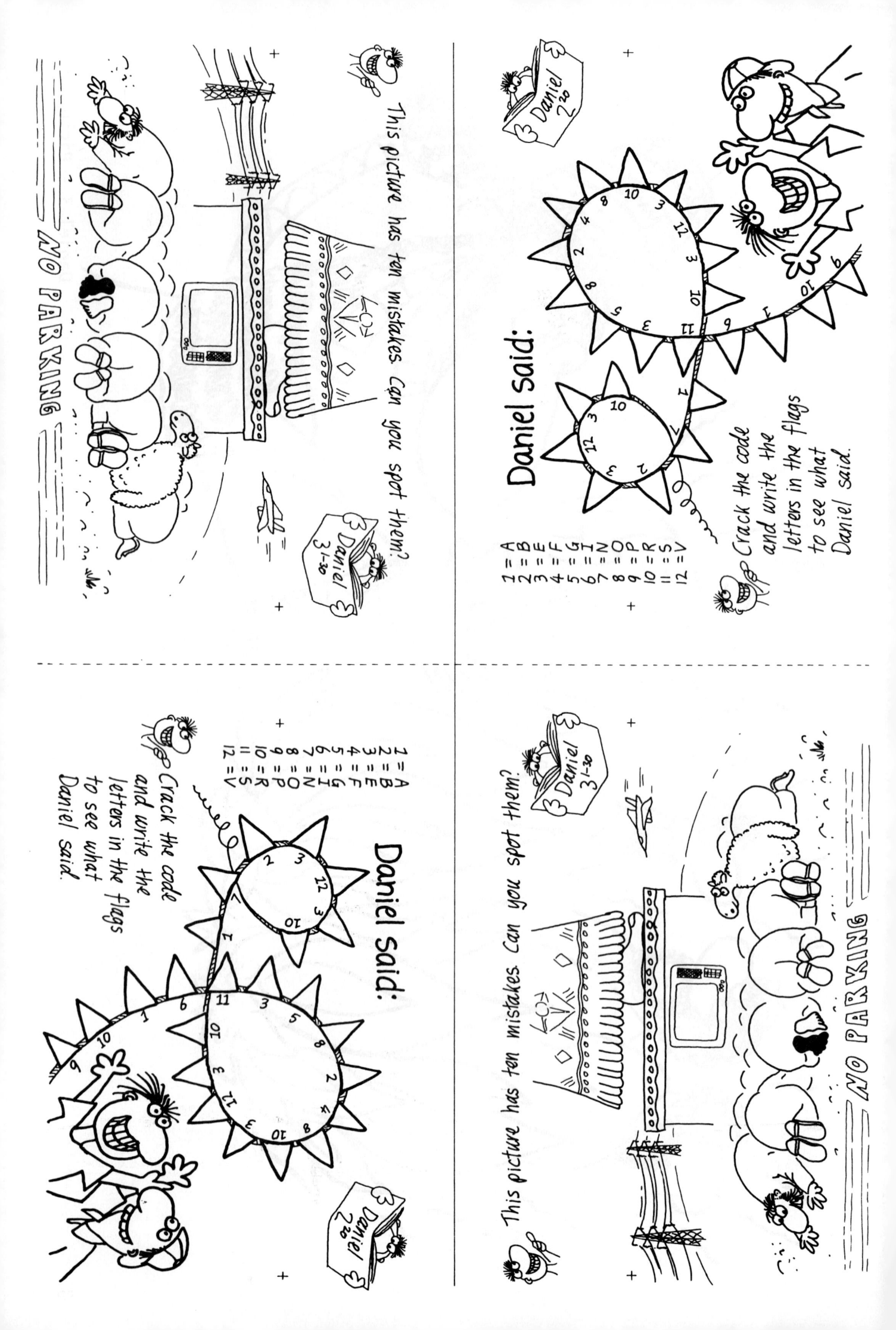

Daniel said:

1 = A
2 = B
3 = E
4 = F
5 = G
6 = I
7 = N
8 = O
9 = P
10 = R
11 = S
12 = V

Crack the code and write the letters in the flags to see what Daniel said.

Daniel said:

1 = A
2 = B
3 = E
4 = F
5 = G
6 = I
7 = N
8 = O
9 = P
10 = R
11 = S
12 = V

Crack the code and write the letters in the flags to see what Daniel said.

This picture has ten mistakes. Can you spot them?

NO PARKING

6 Daniel

LEADERS OVERVIEW

The engine revs and the water-skier sets off at speed towards the slope of the jump ahead...
Exciting stuff, but none of it would be possible without the rope linking the water-skier to the powerful boat!

Even after many years in God's service, Daniel was still facing tough challenges. He had a stark choice: give up prayer for thirty days... or be thrown to the lions. For Daniel there was no option: to live 'detached' from God for any length of time was unthinkable - like water-skiing without a rope! Daniel risked his life to keep the privilege of prayer. Would we do the same?

Many of our children will only be praying when we (or someone else) ask them to... this session asks them to think about choosing to make time for God in their everyday lives.

Clearly, prayer was no empty ritual for Daniel... Ask God, by His Spirit, to water the seeds of a desire to meet with Him in the hearts of every child in your group. Also, PRAY especially for children from not-yet-Christian homes: that they would be able to find time and space for this.

We Would Like Our Children to...

... consider choosing to pray in their own time.

Key Verse

God rescues and saves people and does mighty miracles in heaven and on earth.
Daniel 6:27

Bible Base

Daniel 6:1-28
(Daniel and the Lions)

> To highlight the idea of choosing in this session, try to offer your children choices wherever possible throughout the programme (eg let them decide which picture to do for the story...).

Crucial!

As your children will need time to get the illustrations ready to PRESENT THE BIBLE BASE, we have not included an activity to SET THE SCENE in this session!

Present the Bible Base

Option A: Cartoon Strip - Easy Version!

In advance, photocopy the pictures on pages 65 to 70. You will need one for every two to three children, so cut out the individual characters to make enough to go round if necessary!

1. Ask your children to get into pairs **or** threes.

2. Give each pair one of the photocopied pictures.

3. Ask each pair to colour **and/or** collage the picture they have.

4. Go to point 4 below!

You will need:
to make copies
pencils
coloured pens
a length of wallpaper
  or something similar!
glue

You may need:
scrap materials

Option B: Cartoon Strip - More Artistically Demanding Version!

In advance, look through the story and pick out the main incidents. Write each one out on a separate piece of paper, eg 'some people plot to destroy Daniel', 'King Darius signs a new law', 'Daniel goes to his room to pray' ...and so on. You will need one 'caption' for every two to three children.

1. Ask your children to get into pairs **or** threes.

2. Give each pair one of the captions and some paper.

3. Ask each pair to draw and colour a large picture to go with the caption they have.

4. Now have each picture stuck in the right order(!) along the back of the wallpaper and roll it up carefully...

5. ...Tell the story, using the paraphrase on page 64 as a basis - unroll the wallpaper to reveal the pictures as you go along!

You will need:
to prepare 'captions'
paper
pencils
coloured pens
a length of wallpaper
  or something similar!
glue

You may need:
scrap materials

Focus...

Either in small groups **or** altogether, ask questions to bring out the main points, such as:

➤ *What new law did the king make?*

➤ *What choice did Daniel have to make?*

[Help your children really understand the choice: to give up praying for just 30 days... or face certain death!]

➤ *Why do you think Daniel chose to carry on praying three times a day (even though he knew he would be thrown to the lions...!)?*

[Highlight how important prayer must have been to Daniel. Bring out possible reasons why, eg he really loved God (we would find it hard not to talk with someone we love for a month!); he put God first; he depended on God for help, advice and power ...and so on.]

Pray!

You will need:
to make a 'prayer clock'
suitable pens

In advance, choose **how** you want to pray from LEARNING TO PRAY on pages vii to x. Also, make a 'prayer clock': draw round a dinner plate (*or* similar) on stiff paper *or* card and cut it out. Cut a 'clock hand' from a different coloured card and attach it to the centre of the 'clock face' with a split pin. Don't add numbers! You will need one 'clock' for each prayer group.

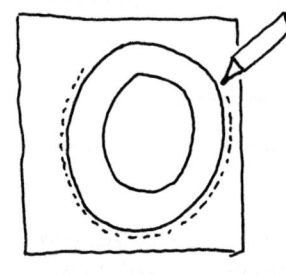

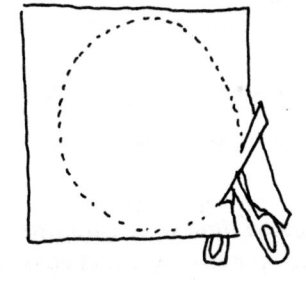

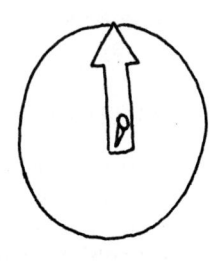

1. Have your children get into small groups with a leader in each group.

2. Within the groups, go round asking each child to finish this sentence: *'If I could choose, I would spend more time ....'* (eg 'watching TV' 'playing basketball'...). If you have time, do the same with: *'If I could choose, I would spend less time ....'* (eg 'at school' 'helping around the house'...).

[Keep it fast-moving!]

3. Now ask: **what are you going to spend time doing next week?** Write **or** draw each activity on the 'clock face' (**or** have the children themselves do this).

4. Remind your children about Daniel by saying something like: *'Daniel chose to pray every day because he knew that spending time with God is the very best thing to do. We can choose to spend time talking with God, too - we could start this week...!'* Add 'talking with God' to your 'prayer clock'.

[Develop this idea as appropriate to your children!]

cont'd.....

5. **NOW PRAY!** Base your prayer-time on the idea you have chosen from pages vii to x. Use the 'prayer clock' as appropriate, eg:

- ask a child to choose an activity by turning the 'clock hand' to point to it! Then pray a short, specific prayer for your children as they are involved in that particular activity this week. Have everyone join in with 'Amen' at the end. Then ask another child to choose... and so on.

- give one of the children the 'clock'. Ask him/her to choose an activity by turning the 'clock hand' to point to it... he/she prays a short prayer about that activity, then passes the 'clock' to the next person... and so on round!

[Make sure that 'talking with God' is included!]

Extra Teaching

Prayer Notes

In advance, prepare the 'prayer notes' on page 71 - see page 4 for guidance!

1. Give each child one of the folded 'prayer notes'.

2. Ask your children to complete and colour the picture, and complete the key verse on the other half of the sheet.

3. As appropriate to your group of children, also ask them to...

   ... **think of things they will be doing this week,** then write **or** draw them inside their 'prayer notes';

   ... **choose to spend time with God this week,** then write **or** draw themselves doing this (place and time) inside their 'prayer notes'.

4. Finally, ask your youngsters to add this session's 'prayer notes' to the rest by threading the string through the two holes and tying it at the front.

You will need:
to prepare the 'prayer notes'
coloured pens **or** pencils

Quiz

In advance, make two large copies of the cartoon lion on page 67. Colour them both and cut them out. Also, draw the letters on separate pieces of paper: you will need eight 'r', four 'o' and four 'a'. Tack the lions on a board _or_ wall. Then tack up the letters next to each lion's mouth to spell 'roar' - twice!

You will need:
to prepare the lions and letters
Blu-tack
scissors
a thick pen
small prizes ('Lion bars'?)!

1. Ask your children to get into two teams.

2. Explain: **'the first team to silence the lion's roar, wins!'**

3. Ask the questions on this and the previous two sessions (page 72) to each team in turn - for each correct answer, change the letters in **roar** as follows:

   1. move the first **r** to the end ➜ **oarr**!
   2. cut off the top of the **a** to make a **u** ➜ **ourr**!
   3. draw a line down the side of the **o** to make a **p** ➜ **purr**!!

4. Repeat with the second roar!

Extra Activities

LET'S FACE IT...

You may need:
the 'Bible base' pictures to jog memories!
poster-sized paper
suitable pens

Daniel, Shadrach, Meshach and Abednego faced enormous pressure to do things which they knew to be wrong... The circumstances and issues will obviously be different, but our children also face pressure to do things they know are not right. This drama activity gives them the chance to think about the choices they have and will give them practical help to do the right thing!

1. Talk together about things children might be persuaded to do which they know to be wrong (eg joining in bullying, taking something from a shop...). Link this with the stories of Daniel, Shadrach, Meshach and Abednego as appropriate.

2. Now have your children get into small friendship groups...

3. Explain the activity: **'we would like each group to make up a short play about a time like that. Show what other people do to try to make one person do the wrong thing...** (give examples, such as "I won't be your friend if you don't..."). **Don't act out what the person chooses to do - 'freeze' when he/she is just about to make up his/her mind!'**

4. Watch each play in turn - when it comes to the crunch, ask: **what do you think he/she should do?**

5. ...Help your children come up with realistic ways out of situations like these - be ready with ideas of your own (including prayer!)! You may wish to write these up as you go along to help your children really grasp them!

To Tie This in:

It was really hard for Daniel and his friends to do the right thing... it might be hard for us too, but when we choose to do what is right by God, He will be with us!

ESCAPE FROM THE DEN

1. Establish one corner of your room as the 'lions' den'... have leaders **or** helpers there to be 'lions'!

2. Also, choose a child to be 'Daniel' and ask him/her to stand in the 'den'... have everyone else go to 'safety' at the opposite end of the room.

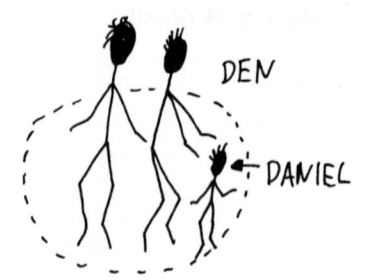

3. Explain the game: **'you have to rescue 'Daniel' from the 'lions' den'! To rescue him/her, somebody has to go right into the 'den', grab 'Daniel's' hand and run with him/her back to 'safety'. It is safe to move closer to the 'den' when the 'lions' backs are turned... but, when the 'lions' turn around, they capture anyone they see moving and take them back to their 'den' - and then you'll have to rescue them too!'**

   ['Lions' can turn round at any time, but not so often that they make any rescue impossible!]

4. Run the game, choosing other 'Daniels' to keep things going if no-one is caught!

To Tie This in:

Would your children honestly have chosen to go into a real lions' den to save someone?! When Daniel had to choose between the lions' den and giving up prayer for 30 days, he chose the lions' den... this just goes to show how special prayer is!

You will need:
plenty of space!

DANIEL AND THE LIONS MOBILE

In advance, photocopy the Daniel figures and lions on page 73 onto thin card - you will need four lions and one Daniel for each mobile! Also, do some of the stages below if your children are likely to find the whole thing a bit much!

1. Cut out and colour the lions and the Daniel figure.

2. Make a hole at the bottom of each lion - thread through a length of wool, then knot it at the end and fray it to make a tail.

You will need:
to prepare the figures
scissors
coloured pens **or** pencils
yellow **or** orange wool
garden cane **or** dowelling, cut into lengths of about 30cms; **or** paper, rolled tightly lengthways
light-coloured (but strong) thread
sticky tape

3. Take two lengths of cane **or** dowelling **or** rolled-up paper - place them in an X shape and secure it with tape.

4. Attach lengths of the light-coloured thread to the back of each lion and Daniel figure.

5. Assemble the mobile!

To Tie This in:

The lions do not touch Daniel in the middle of the mobile... Remember that God stopped the lions from touching Daniel in the den - isn't God great?!

ADDITIONAL IDEAS:

1. Have your children make lion masks from papier mâché **or** 'modroc'; **or** make lion faces with face paints!

2. Have your children make clocks! You can buy simple clock mechanisms quite cheaply from good art and craft suppliers. Then help your children paint a design for the clock face on a piece of plastic **or** board. Keeping this at home will help remind them about what they are choosing to do with their time...!

DANIEL 6:1-28
– A PARAPHRASE...

As Daniel looked down into the darkness, he could see the lions beginning to stir. He heard angry growling... then a terrifying roar. Behind him, a huge stone was being pushed across the entrance to the lions' den - there was no escape......!

It had all started earlier that week. The new king, Darius, wanted to put Daniel in charge of the whole kingdom. This made some people jealous, so they looked for ways of getting Daniel into trouble. They watched him carefully to see if he was lazy... but he never was; they tried to catch him being dishonest... but he never lied or cheated. Daniel was <u>always</u> trustworthy. Then one of them hit on an idea:
"I know what his weakness is!"
"What?"
"His God! Daniel would do anything rather than let His God down in any way! Let's get King Darius to make a law forbidding anybody to pray for the next 30 days. That will finish Daniel!"

And they did. King Darius signed the law and announced that anybody who prayed to anyone except him in the next 30 days would be thrown to the lions.

When Daniel heard about the new law, he thought carefully: what should he do? Three times every day Daniel went to his room to pray and thank God - should he stop praying to God just for the next thirty days.... or carry on praying and risk being thrown into the lions den?

● *If you were Daniel's friend, what would you advise him to do?*
In fact, it wasn't a hard decision. Daniel wanted to serve the king, but God would always come first! Besides, he knew that it was stupid to try to do his important job without asking God for help and advice. And what's more, Daniel could not bear the thought of not being able to spend time with God every day. So, he decided to carry on praying like he always did. And, of course, when the men saw him, they went straight to the king......

So now here he was, alone with fierce and hungry lions.
"May your God protect you from the lions!" shouted King Darius, as the stone was pushed across the entrance of the den.

King Darius had always admired and trusted Daniel. He was very upset when he realised that his silly law would mean that Daniel, of all people, would die. He went home, and did not eat or sleep all night.

At dawn, King Darius got up and ran to the lions' den. He knew nobody could survive alone with those lions, but he felt strangely hopeful as he got closer and closer...
"Daniel!" he shouted, "You serve the living God - has He been able to protect you from the lions?"
From deep inside the den he heard a voice: "Good morning, your majesty! The lions have not hurt me, because God sent an angel to close their mouths!"

Later, the king wrote a letter to everyone in his kingdom:
"Daniel's God is the living God! His God will live for ever and His Kingdom will never be destroyed! God will always rule over the whole universe! He saves people and does amazing things, like protecting Daniel from the lions. From now on, everyone in the whole kingdom must respect Daniel's God!"
And Daniel was successful in all he did, because he trusted God.

Daniel 6 - Picture 1

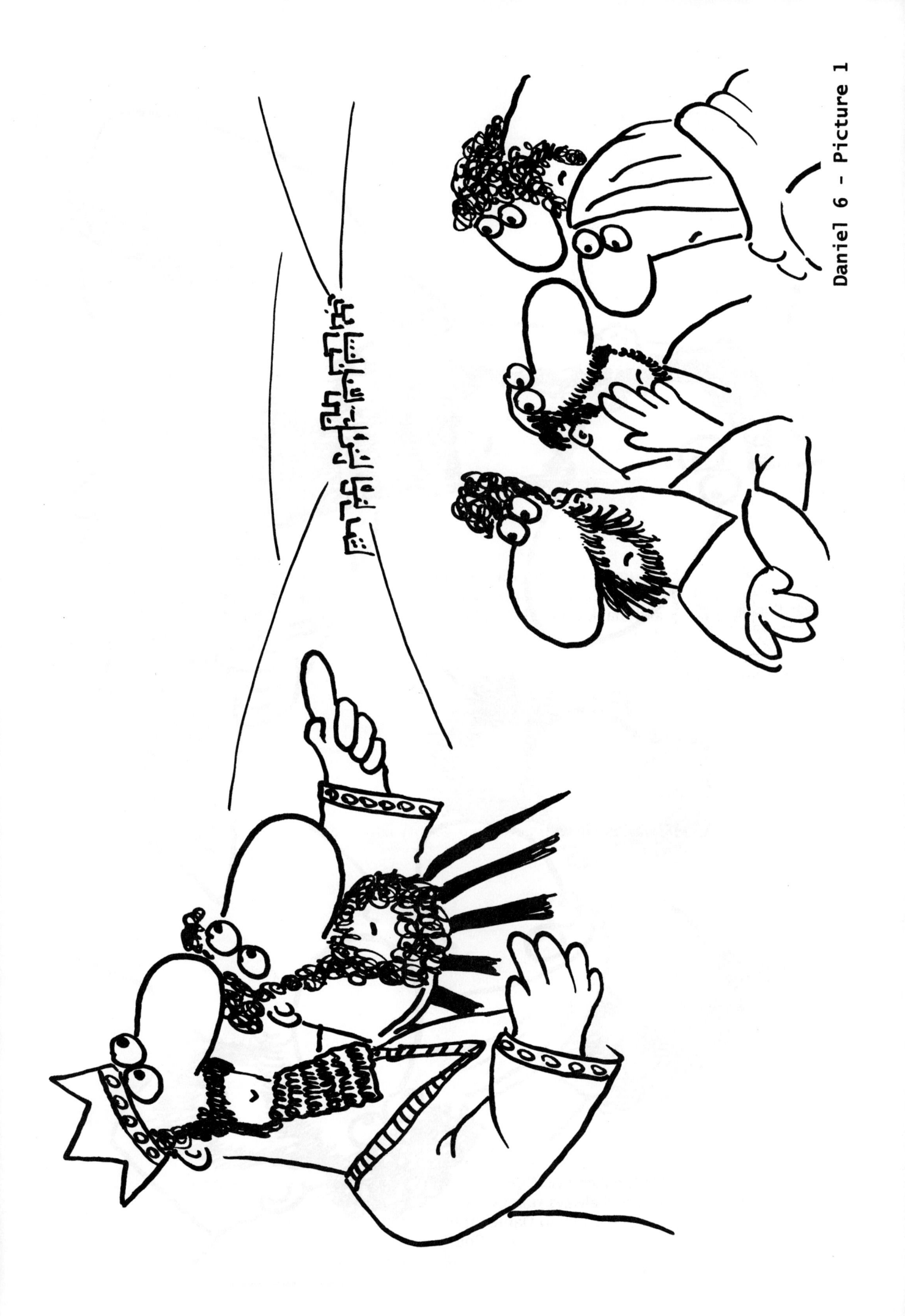

Daniel 6 - Picture 2

Daniel 6 - Picture 3

Daniel 6 - Picture 4

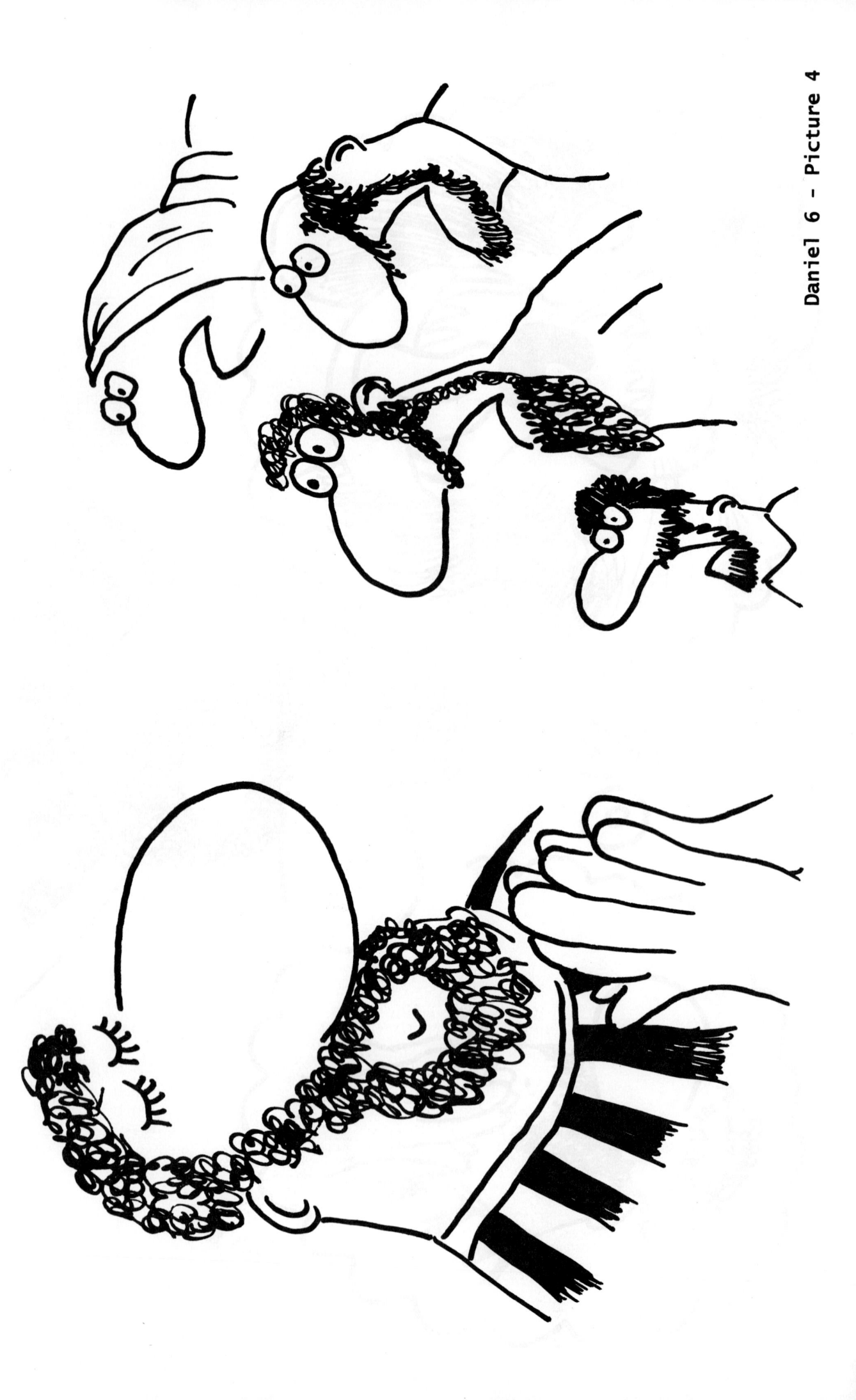

Daniel 6 - Picture 5

Daniel 6 - Picture 6

Activity Sheet (4 panels)

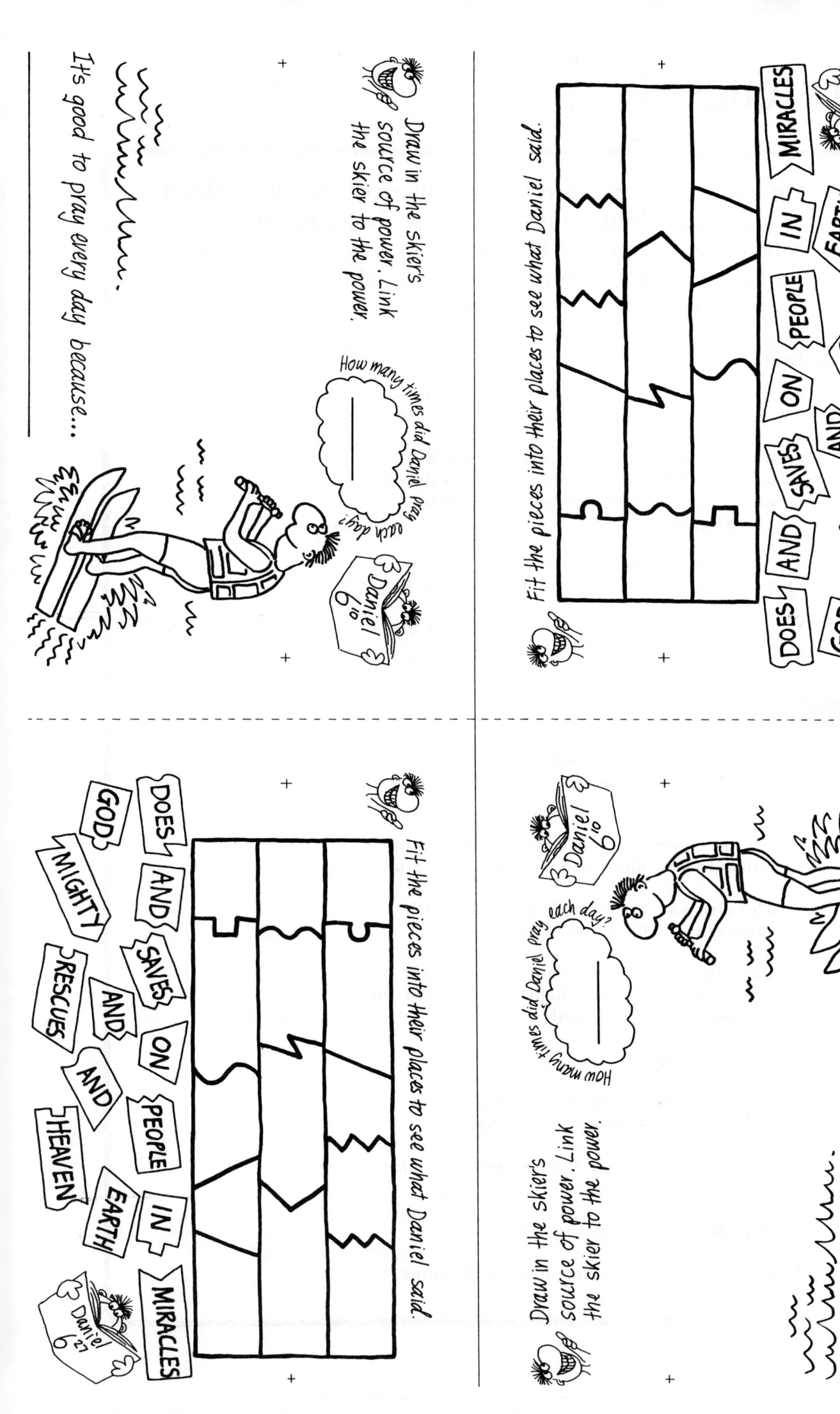

Panel 1 (top right)

Fit the pieces into their places to see what Daniel said.

[Puzzle with pieces labeled:]
GOD — DOES — AND — SAVES — AND — RESCUES — MIGHTY — ON — PEOPLE — AND — IN — EARTH — HEAVEN — MIRACLES

Daniel 6

Panel 2 (top left)

Draw in the skier's source of power. Link the skier to the power.

How many times did Daniel pray each day? ____

Daniel 6

It's good to pray every day because...
_____

Panel 3 (bottom right)

Draw in the skier's source of power. Link the skier to the power.

How many times did Daniel pray each day? ____

Daniel 6

It's good to pray every day because...
_____

Panel 4 (bottom left)

Fit the pieces into their places to see what Daniel said.

[Puzzle with pieces labeled:]
GOD — DOES — AND — SAVES — AND — RESCUES — MIGHTY — ON — PEOPLE — AND — IN — EARTH — HEAVEN — MIRACLES

Daniel 6

QUIZ QUESTIONS

Please read these through in advance and adapt them to suit your children if necessary! Some of the questions have more than one answer, so decide what you are going to accept as correct - children have a very strong sense of fairness!

Session 4

Your Answers!

1. What did King Nebucadnezzar want his magicians and advisers to find out for him? _____

2. When the magicians and advisers were unable to tell him the meaning of his dream, what did King Nebuchadnezzar order his guards to do? _____

3. Daniel came to the rescue... but what did Shadrach, Meshach and Abednego do to help? _____

4. Who could tell the king the meaning of his dream? _____

Session 5

1. What did King Nebuchadnezzar order everyone to do when they heard the sound of music? _____

2. Why did Shadrach, Meshach and Abednego refuse to bow down and worship the statue? _____

3. Who else was in the flaming furnace with Shadrach, Meshach and Abednego? _____

4. What did King Nebuchadnezzar say about God when He rescued Shadrach, Meshach and Abednego from the flaming furnace? _____

Session 6

1. Why did some people try to get Daniel in trouble with the new king, Darius? _____

2. What did King Darius' law say people could not do for 30 days? _____

3. Why did Daniel break the law? _____

4. Why wasn't Daniel eaten alive by the lions? _____

73

7 Jesus

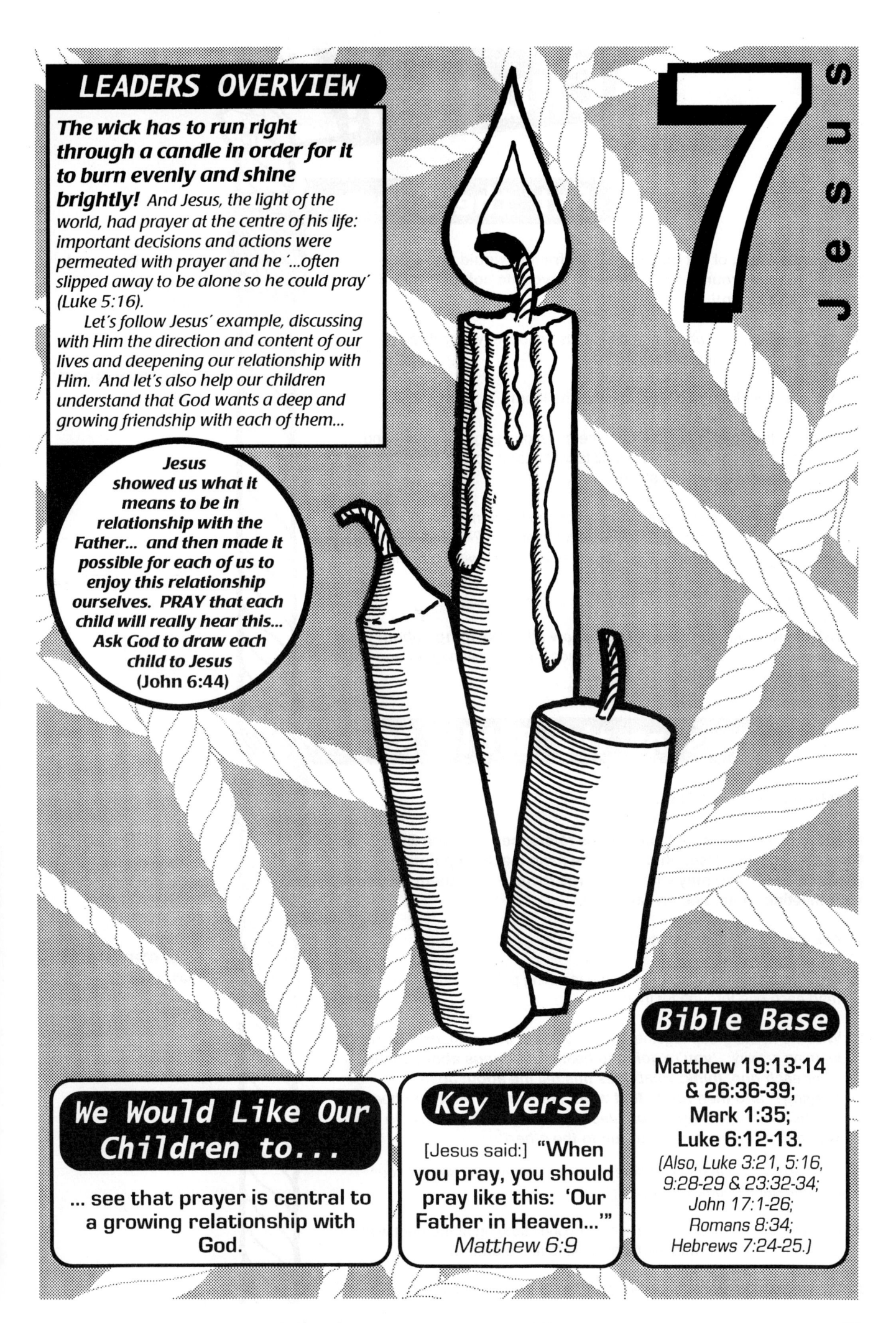

LEADERS OVERVIEW

The wick has to run right through a candle in order for it to burn evenly and shine brightly! And Jesus, the light of the world, had prayer at the centre of his life: important decisions and actions were permeated with prayer and he '...often slipped away to be alone so he could pray' (Luke 5:16).

Let's follow Jesus' example, discussing with Him the direction and content of our lives and deepening our relationship with Him. And let's also help our children understand that God wants a deep and growing friendship with each of them...

Jesus showed us what it means to be in relationship with the Father... and then made it possible for each of us to enjoy this relationship ourselves. PRAY that each child will really hear this... Ask God to draw each child to Jesus (John 6:44)

We Would Like Our Children to...

... see that prayer is central to a growing relationship with God.

Key Verse

[Jesus said:] "When you pray, you should pray like this: 'Our Father in Heaven...'"
Matthew 6:9

Bible Base

Matthew 19:13-14 & 26:36-39;
Mark 1:35;
Luke 6:12-13.
(Also, Luke 3:21, 5:16, 9:28-29 & 23:32-34; John 17:1-26; Romans 8:34; Hebrews 7:24-25.)

Crucial!

Set the Scene

In advance, think of six questions only friends would know the answer to (eg favourite football team? favourite colour? birthday? pets? ...and so on)!

1. Ask for volunteers who are good friends - choose two <u>or</u> three pairs who know each other well.

2. Ask one child from each pair to leave the room.

3. Now ask the child left in the room the questions <u>about his/her friend</u>, (ie what is <u>his/her</u> favourite football team? ...and so on). Make a note of the answers as you go along.

4. Have the other children return and ask them the same questions <u>about themselves</u>, (ie what is <u>your</u> favourite football team? ...and so on). When this answer is what their friend said earlier, award a point!

5. The pair with the most points, wins!

6. Ask the winning pair: **how did you know all those things about your partner?** Bring out the ideas that friends talk with each other and are interested in each other.

You will need:
to prepare the questions!
notepaper
a pen

You may need:
small prizes!

Present the Bible Base

Option A: Active!

In advance, choose about eight of the references from the Bible Base on page 75. Also, photocopy the main teaching points on pages 82 to 83 (you may wish to enlarge them) - tack them around your meeting room, one on each wall.

1. Ask everyone to find a partner.

2. Draw your children's attention to the teaching points around the walls - read each one through for them.

3. With the whole group together in the middle of the room, explain this learning activity: *'you're going to hear eight things about Jesus... after each one, think: what does this tell me about Jesus praying? and then run to that wall! Sometimes what you hear will tell you two things about Jesus praying... so you run to one wall and get your partner to run to the other!'*

   [Perhaps do the first one altogether as a 'dummy run', so that your children get the idea!]

4. Run the activity! Put a sticker on everyone standing at the right wall each time - the pair with the most stickers at the end, wins!

5. With the whole group together again, recap the main points.

You will need:
to make copies
to choose the verses
Blu-tack
small stickers

You may need:
small prizes!

You will need:
to prepare the verses
or references

Option B: Drama

In advance, *either* make a copy of the verses on page 81 and cut along the dotted lines as shown; *or* select a number of the references from the Bible Base on page 75, write them out on separate pieces of paper and have Bibles at the ready!

1. Ask your children to get into four groups (**or** into as many groups as you have references!).

2. Give each group one of the texts **or** references.

3. Now have each group work out how to simply dramatise the text.

4. With everyone together again, have each group in turn read and act out its text...

5. ...After each one, bring out the appropriate points, eg:

   - **Jesus prayed for people He met** - such as children, everyone who follows him (and that includes us now!) and even those who hurt Him...

   - **Jesus prayed before doing things** - such as choosing, going to different places, healing, helping and teaching...

   - **Jesus prayed in sad and hard times** - such as when He knew that He was going to be arrested...

   - **Jesus made time to pray.**

Focus...

You will need:
a candle
matches

1. Light the candle.

2. Talk about how important the wick is... point out that it has to run the whole way through the middle of the candle; it's no good just having a bit here and there!

3. Make the link with prayer by saying something like:

   - *'Jesus had prayer right at the centre of his whole life. He prayed very often about all sorts of different things... Jesus was just used to talking everything over with His Father in heaven;*

   - *if we just pray every now and then, perhaps when someone tells us to, we're missing out on something really special!! Prayer is a crucial part of the deep friendship we can have with God... it's like talking things over with the very closest friend.'*

   [The fact that God is 'our Father in heaven' is powerful: if you use it here, be aware that it may be an obstacle for any children who have problems with their earthly dad.]

Pray!

In advance, choose <u>how</u> you want to pray from LEARNING TO PRAY on pages vii to x. Also, get together a set of 'props' to represent the different parts of a typical day for your children, (eg a packet of cereal for breakfast, a bus pass for travel, books <u>or</u> pencils for school...). Put them all in a box <u>or</u> bin-liner.

You will need:
a set of 'props'
a box <u>or</u> bin-liner

1. Remind your children about Jesus' (and Daniel's!) prayers by saying something like: *'Jesus prayed at all times of the day about all sorts of things... and He would love us to do the same!'*

2. Invite individuals to take out one 'prop' at a time and ask: *which part of your day does this remind you of?*

3. Talk together about praying at each different time - ask: *what sorts of things could we talk with God about first thing in the morning?* ...and so on.

4. Spread the 'props' around the room...

5. **NOW PRAY!** Base your prayer-time on the idea you have chosen from pages vii to x. Move round as a whole group <u>or</u> in small groups and pray at each 'prop' about the part of the day it represents, eg:

   - help your children choose a prayer for each part of their day from a published prayer book - then pray them together when you get to that 'prop';

   - ask your children (in pairs <u>or</u> three's) to write a prayer for a particular part of their day - then pray them together when you get to that 'prop';

   - simply invite your children to pray short, unrehearsed prayers at each 'prop'!

Extra Teaching

Prayer in my Life...

In advance, ask about three people to come ready to talk about prayer in their own lives - your regular helpers and co-leaders would be fine, but someone of around your children's age would make a special impact! Also, think up and write out a few questions to bring out the points you want to emphasise, eg *why do you pray? When do you pray? Is it always easy to pray?* ...and so on.

You will need:
to brief some prayer 'role-models'!

1. Simply 'interview' each of your 'guests' (<u>or</u> have some of your children do this!) - highlight any comments about the person's relationship with God.

2. Have a clear opportunity, **<u>either</u>** in small groups **<u>or</u>** more informally to talk with your children about the 'interviews' - help them begin to see how a relationship with God **<u>and/or</u>** a regular prayer-time could work out in their own lives.

Prayer Notes

You will need:
to prepare the 'prayer notes'
coloured pens **or** pencils

Answers:
Jesus prayed; God; helping; healing; choosing; teaching; disciples; children; himself; day

In advance, prepare the 'prayer notes' on page 84 - see page 4 for guidance!

1. Give each child one of the folded 'prayer notes'.

2. Ask your children to do the puzzle, colour the picture and complete the key verse on the other half of the sheet.

3. As appropriate to your group of children, also ask them to...

   ... write **or** draw a ***prayer for a particular part of their day or week*** inside their 'prayer notes';

   ... respond in words **or** pictures to ***the idea of being friends with God***.

4. Finally, ask your children to add this session's 'prayer notes' to the rest by threading the string through the two holes and tying it at the front.

Extra Activities

CANDLE DECORATING

You will need:
a 'nightlight' per child
large white stickers
stickers (different colours and shapes)
coloured pens

1. Give everyone a 'nightlight'.

2. Put out a selection of stickers and pens for your children to use to decorate their 'nightlight' - they might begin by colouring **and/or** writing on the white stickers and then wrapping them around the 'nightlight'.

3. If appropriate, suggest that your children put their nightlights somewhere as a reminder to talk with God this week...

ALTERNATIVE IDEA:
If you have time, candlemaking would also be a great activity. You can buy kits **and/or** the equipment from good craft and toy shops. It would be best to run this in small groups on a rota basis... and please make sure that your children are very carefully supervised throughout!

To Tie This in:

The wick has to run right through the middle of the 'nightlight'... Jesus' life had prayer right at the centre, because He loved to talk everything over with his Father in heaven... and He would love us to learn to do the same!

(PRAYER) WRIST-BAND

In advance, cut 20cm lengths of cord (the bright, shoelace-type is good for this!) _or_ leather thong - enough for one per child.

1. Simply let your children choose beads to thread onto a length of cord to tie around their wrists! If you would them to use this as a prayer-prompt, how about asking them to pick...

   - three beads only - one for 'thanks', one for 'sorry' and one for 'please';
   - a bead to represent each person **or** situation they would like to talk with God about?

2. As appropriate, suggest that your children pray whenever they become aware of their wrist-bands this week...

To Tie This in:

The cord has to run right through the middle of each bead... Jesus' life had prayer right at the centre, because He loved to talk everything over with his Father in heaven... and He would love us to learn to do the same!

You will need:
lengths of cord _or_ leather thong
beads

POLO RACE

In advance, set up two simple 'obstacle courses' by passing string over, under and around one or two chairs, leaving both ends hanging loose.

1. Ask the children to get into two equal-sized teams.

2. Explain the game: *'everyone is going to get a polo! The idea is to get your polo to the end of the obstacle course without breaking it! When I say 'go', the first person from each team will thread the string through his/her polo, and then move the polo along and over the obstacles. When he/she has reached the first chair, the second person can go. The team with the most whole polos at the end, wins!'*

[In the event of a tie, the fastest team wins!]

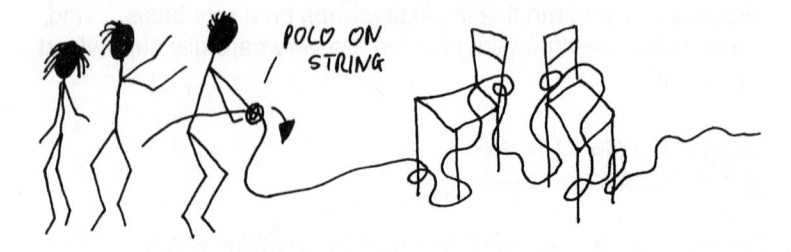

3. Give everyone a polo and run the game!

To Tie This in:

This game is only possible with polos... other sweets don't have any room for the string to go through! Being friends with God is so special and important that we need to make room for prayer in our lives!

You will need:
to set up the 'obstacle courses'
two packets of polos

You may need:
small prizes!

Then the people brought their little children to Jesus

so he could put this hands on them

and pray for them.

MATTHEW 19:13

At that time Jesus went off to a mountain to pray,
and he spent the night praying to God.
The next morning, Jesus called his followers
to him and chose twelve of them...

LUKE 6:12-13

[Jesus] said to them, "Sit here while I go over there
and pray." ...He began to be very sad and troubled.
He said to them, "My heart is full of sorrow,
to the point of death..."

MATTHEW 26:36-39

Early the next morning, while it was still dark,

Jesus woke and left the house.

He went to a lonely place, where he prayed.

MARK 1:35

Jesus prayed before doing things

Jesus prayed for people he met

Jesus made time to pray!

Cockadoodledooo!

Jesus prayed in sad and hard times

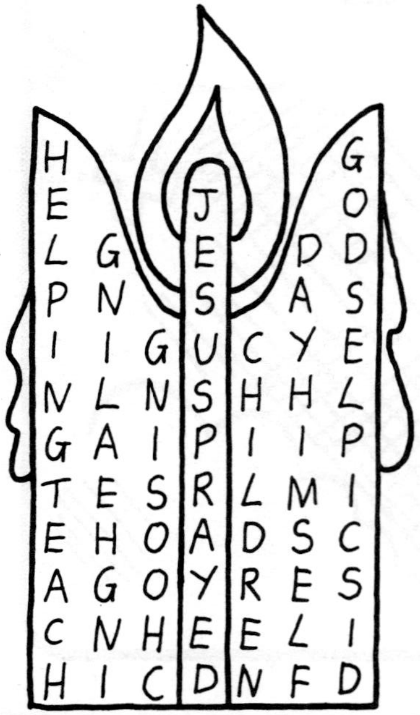

Heaven...

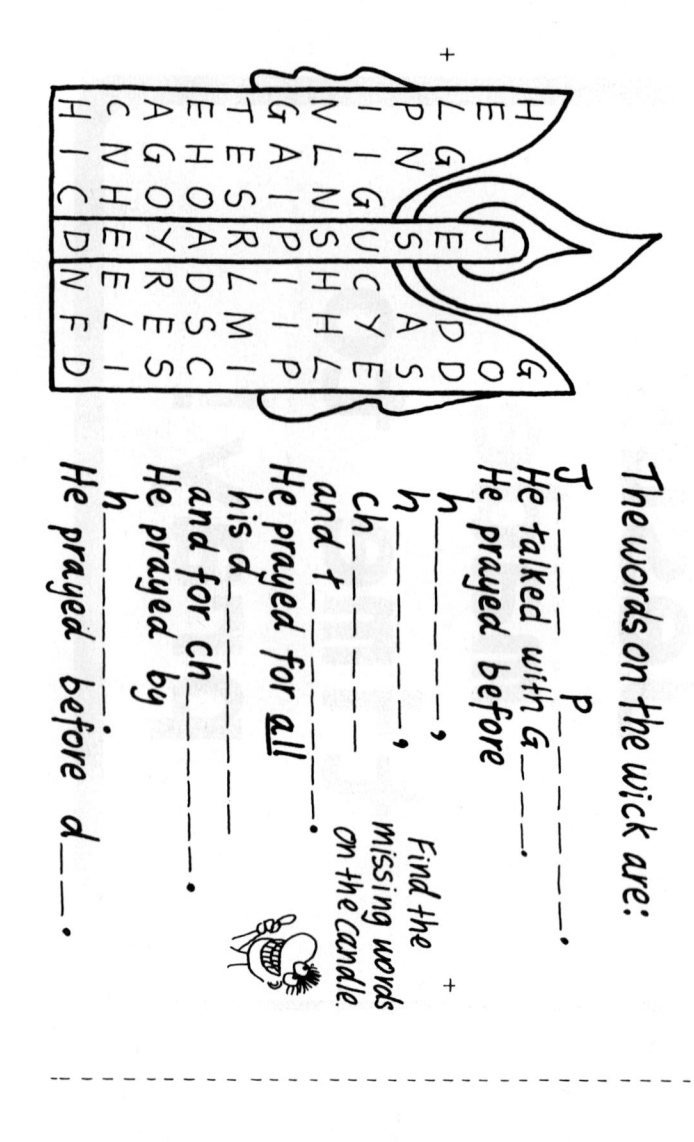

Our father in like this:
When you should pray

📖 *Matthew 6:9*

▶ Put a mirror or a piece of shiny paper alongside here to read something Jesus said!

Then write it here ▶

....
....
....
....

The words on the wick are:

J— P—
He talked with G—
He prayed before
h—,
h—
ch—
and t—,
He prayed for all
his d—
and for ch—
He prayed by
h—
He prayed before d—.

Find the missing words on the candle.

Word search grid (on candle):
H E G J G O D D
L P N S E A S H
I G U C Y E
V L N S H L I P
G A I P L M
T E S R L M I P
E H O A D S C
A G O Y R E S I
C N H E E L I
H I C D N F D

When you should pray
is like this:
Our father in
Heaven...

▶ Put a mirror or a piece of shiny paper alongside here to read something Jesus said!

Then write it here ▶

📖 *Matthew 6:9*

The words on the wick are:

J— P—
He talked with G—.
He prayed before
h—,
h—
ch—
and t—,
He prayed for all
his d—
and for ch—
He prayed by
h—
He prayed before d—.

Find the missing words on the candle.

Word search grid (on candle):
H E G J G O D D
L P N S E A S H
I G U C Y E
V L N S H L I P
G A I P L M
T E S R L M I P
E H O A D S C
A G O Y R E S I
C N H E E L I
H I C D N F D

LEADERS OVERVIEW

Alone in untamed jungle... the reality may not be as exciting as the films would have us think! Picture the scene: a small group has become hopelessly lost... irresponsible decisions have brought them to a deep ravine which cuts them off from their correct route. The group is in serious trouble, but they carry the solution with them - a rope will bridge the gap: it will take courage to use, but it is strong and reliable.

When our selfishness cuts us off from God, there is always a way back through Jesus. The word 'sorry' bridges the widest gulf! It may be hard to admit our sin and to pray for forgiveness, but the joy it brings is wonderful!

The woman who anointed Jesus did not use words, but her actions spoke volumes. What a contrast to the self-satisfied Pharisee, who completely missed the point and so missed out! Let's help our children see that it's really good to own up to God about the things we do wrong and so be forgiven by Him... we will then focus next session on the cross, which makes it all possible!

The woman was acutely aware of her own sin and immensely grateful for the love and forgiveness Jesus showed her... Ask God, by his Holy Spirit, to gently help your children see their need to own up and be sorry (John 16:8-9), and then to know how good it is to be forgiven!

8
Jesus

We Would Like Our Children to...
... understand that prayer for forgiveness is a crucial part of our relationship with God.

Key Verse
If we confess our sins, he will forgive our sins.
1 John 1:9

Bible Base
Luke 7:36-50
(A Woman Washes Jesus' Feet)

Crucial!

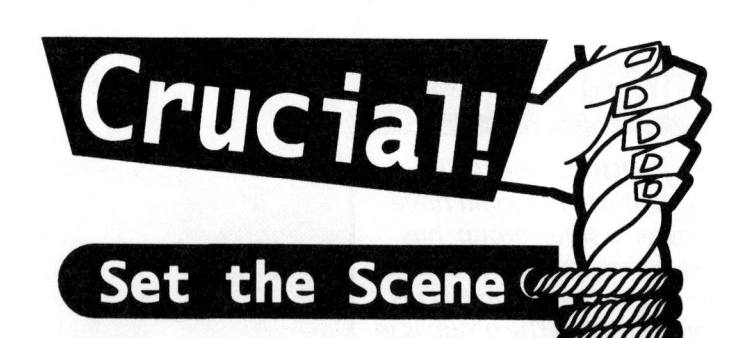

Set the Scene

1. **Either** altogether **or** in small groups, ask: **who would you like to invite round to your house (or here) as a special guest?** Encourage your children to think of someone important to them, who might be famous **or** a friend **or** family member....

2. ...Now talk together about what your children would do to welcome their guest from the moment he/she arrived - help them think of the obvious (eg open the door, take their coat, show them where to sit...)! Perhaps have them act this out as they describe it.

   [If you have children in your group from different cultural backgrounds, it would be good to compare customs and enjoy the differences!]

3. End by showing what was customary in Jesus' day - again, perhaps act this out with a co-leader, ie
   - kiss the guest on the cheek;
   - offer him/her a bowl of water to wash his/her feet;
   - pour oil on his/her head;
   - show him/her a cushion to lie on;
   - probably leave the door open!

4. See what your children think of this, then lead straight into...

You will need:
a bowl of water
oil (cooking **or** body, **not** engine!)
cushions

Present the Bible Base

Option A: Faces

In advance, *either* make one copy of the faces on page 92 on OHP acetate *or* make photocopies, enough for one between two.

1. Show the OHP acetate **or** hand out the photocopies and pens: to help your children get the idea, just ask a few quick questions about the faces, eg **how do you think this person is feeling? Which face looks angry?** ...and so on.

2. Tell the story, using the paraphrase on page 93 as a basis...

3. ...Pause to ask your children to think about how the different characters might be feeling, as suggested on page 93 - **either** ask one child to circle one (or more) of the faces on the OHP **or** give your children time to choose faces from their own copies.

You will need:
to make a copy(ies)
suitable pens

Option B: Hearts

In advance, cut two large hearts out of paper. Write 'Simon' on one and 'the woman' on the other. Tack them side by side on a board **or** wall.

1. Tell the story, using the paraphrase on page 93 as a basis...

You will need:
to prepare the hearts
Blu-tack
suitable pens

2. ...Pause at various points and ask: **what do you think he/she is feeling in his/her heart?** Have your children's ideas written on the heart-shapes as you go along.

3. At the end, talk together about which heart made Jesus happy - and why.

Focus...

Either in small groups **or** altogether, ask questions to bring out the main points, such as:

➤ *What did the woman do to Jesus?*

[Help your children recall that she cried, washed Jesus' feet with her tears, dried them with her hair, kissed them and poured perfume on them.]

➤ *What did she want to show Jesus by doing this?*

[Bring out ideas, eg she was sad about the things she had done wrong in her life, she was thankful that Jesus had forgiven her, she loved Him very much ...and so on.)

Pray!

You will need:
to prepare this...

In advance, choose **how** you want to pray from LEARNING TO PRAY on pages vii to x. Also, look ahead to SPEAKING WITHOUT WORDS in EXTRA TEACHING overleaf... if this is appropriate for your children, consider doing it after point 2 below and incorporate it into the prayer time! *Alternatively,* just find something to help your children focus, such as a bottle of perfume **or** candle (to link in with the previous session)...

1. **Either** in small groups **or** altogether, remind your children about this incident by saying something like: *'this woman had so much she wanted to say to Jesus... but she didn't use words. Like her, we can say things to God in our hearts, with our feelings and with actions...'*

2. If appropriate, develop the idea of owning up to God about the things we do wrong:

   ● say something like: *'put your hand up if you've ever done anything wrong! Now put your hand up if you've ever tried to cover up something you've done wrong, (perhaps by hiding something you broke or blaming someone else...)'*

   ● now ask: *what makes it hard to own up to the things which we do wrong?* Bring out ideas about not wanting to get punished!

   ● go on to say something like: *'when Jesus died on the cross, He was punished instead of us! Jesus loves us too much to let us spoil our lives (and other people's!) by the wrong things we say and do. He wants us to own up to God about the things we've done wrong so that He can forgive us...'*

3. Allow time, as appropriate, for God to prompt your children by His Holy Spirit about the things they need to say 'sorry' for now - it may be helpful to give a few examples, but don't make it heavy!

cont'd.....

4. NOW PRAY! Base your prayer-time on the idea you have chosen from pages vii to x, eg:

- create a suitably quiet atmosphere...! Begin and end this prayer time yourself, but leave a gap in the middle for your children to talk with God themselves... Say something like:

  'Dear God, thank you that you love us very much and that your love never, ever stops. We are sorry that we sometimes do things to hurt you and other people. Right now, we want to say 'sorry' for these things........ [QUIET!] .... Thank you, Father God, that you always forgive us when we own up to the wrong things we have done. Amen.'

Include your children's ideas from SPEAKING WITHOUT WORDS, as appropriate.

5. Also, encourage your children to go and say 'sorry' to anyone they have hurt at home, at school, around the streets...

ADDITIONAL IDEA:
Use an extra illustration to show that, once sin is confessed, it is gone for good. Possibilities include:
- writing something on a piece of paper, then carefully burning it;
- writing the first letter of something on a whiteboard, then wiping it away ...and so on.

Extra Teaching

Speaking Without Words

You will need: to prepare this!

In advance, decide what to focus on here: being sorry *or* gratitude *or* love. Choose one *or* a range of ideas to help your children express this without using words. Possibilities include:

- drawing symbols *or* pictures *or* patterns (- help them think about which colours to choose!);
- making figures *or* shapes from clay *or* Blu-tack *or* aluminium foil...
- having groups make 'living sculptures';
- inventing dance sequences;
- composing pieces of music.

Get together the appropriate materials and equipment *and/or* ask your co-leaders to organise and run the different options.

Simply ask your children to choose from the options you have on offer - help them to express being sorry (**or** gratitude **or** love) through the activity. Have an opportunity to see everyone's ideas... perhaps include them in the prayer time, as suggested on the previous page.

Prayer Notes

You will need:
to prepare the 'prayer notes'
coloured pens **or** pencils

<u>Answers:</u>
kiss; foot; perfume; cry.
The word across the rope bridge is: **sorry**!

In advance, prepare the 'prayer notes' on page 91 - see page 4 for guidance!

1. Give each child one of the folded 'prayer notes'.

2. Ask your children to do the puzzle, colour the picture and complete the key verse on the other half of the sheet.

3. Also, ask your children to think of **things they need to say 'sorry' to God for...**

4. ...Ask them to write **or** draw these things inside their 'prayer notes'. Remind your children that you won't be looking at these, but suggest they use a code or symbol if they prefer!

5. Finally, ask your children to add this session's 'prayer notes' to the rest by threading the string through the two holes and tying it at the front.

Extra Activities

TANGLES

1. Ask your children to get into groups of about eight.

2. Ask one child from each group to leave the room **or** turn away, whilst the rest of each group gets into a circle holding hands...

3. ...Now explain the game: *'get your group into a tangle! You can twist around and crawl under somebody else's arms or legs, but keep holding the same two hands the whole time. We'll then ask the other person from your group to come back and try to untangle you. Remember not to let go of anybody's hand whilst you are being untangled... Go!'*

4. Repeat, with different children undoing the tangles each time.

To Tie This in:

Knots and tangles mess things up and are difficult to undo! The things we do wrong are like those tangles ~ they mess things up between us and other people and between us and God... and they are difficult to put right! Owning up to God and letting Him forgive us are crucial parts of putting things right again ('letting God undo the tangle')!

MENDING BROKEN FRIENDSHIPS

In advance, find a video clip _or_ make up a quick drama sketch to show any kind of friction in any kind of relationship! If appropriate, also think of some realistic role-play situations, in which someone does something to spoil a friendship (see point 6 below).

1. Show the video clip **or** perform the drama.

2. **Either** in small groups **or** altogether, ask a few questions, such as: *what's gone wrong in this friendship? Why have things gone wrong? How can things be put right again?*

3. Now ask: *what other things spoil friendships?* Note these down as you go along and be ready to prompt with ideas (eg someone talking about you behind your back; someone saying something unkind; someone taking something which is yours...).

4. Talk sensitively together about how it feels when friends do these things to us... then help your children see that we also do some of these things to our friends!

5. Go on to help your children think through how to mend a friendship when one of these things spoils it! Bring out the following points:

   - say (**or** show) you are sorry;
   - make things right if you can
   - give back something you took or replace something you broke;
   - try not to do it again!

   Highlight the importance of forgiveness in this!

6. If you have time, have your children role-play a friendship being spoilt and then mended again... **or** have them act out what might happen after the video clip **or** drama you used in point 1!

To Tie This in:

The wrong things we do and say have broken our friendship with God, too. Like the woman in the story, we can start to put things right now, by owning up to God about them... He is always ready to forgive and He never stops loving us!

You will need:
a video clip **or** drama sketch
a board **or** OHP **or** poster-sized paper
suitable pens

You may need:
to invent some role-play situations

GETTING CLEAN!

In advance, get hold of some small, sealable glass bottles - supermarkets and household stores sell them quite cheaply as containers for herbs and spices!

Help your children design and paint a bottle, then fill it with bubble bath.

To Tie This in:

This is just to give your children something to remind them of the foot-washing incident! However, you might also use this activity to talk about being washed clean from the things we do wrong (Psalm 51:1-2,7 and Hebrews 10:22)...

You will need:
a large bottle of bubble bath (**or** similar)
plain glass bottles
glass paints
brushes
white spirit

You may need:
a jug **or** funnel

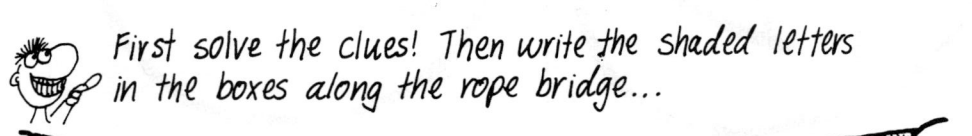

FORGIVENESS
1 2 3 4 5 6 7 8 9

Use the code to find a promise to remember!

$\underline{w}_7 \underline{}\ \underline{c}_2 \underline{}_8 \underline{}_1 \underline{}_7 \underline{}_9 \underline{}_9$ — another word for 'own up'

$\underline{w}_7\ \underline{h}_7\ \underline{w}_5\ \underline{}_1\ \underline{}_1\ \underline{u}_3$

$\underline{}_5\ \underline{}_1\ ,\ \underline{}_9\ \underline{}_5\ \underline{}_8\ \underline{}_9\ \underline{}_1\ \underline{}_2\ \underline{}_3\ \underline{}_4\ \underline{}_5\ \underline{}_6\ \underline{}_7\ \underline{u}_2\ \underline{}_5\ \underline{}_3$

(Look at Psalm 32' to see why it's good to do this!)

1 John 1:9

First solve the clues! Then write the shaded letters in the boxes along the rope bridge...

...Why is this so important?

Luke 7:36-50

First solve the clues! Then write the shaded letters in the boxes along the rope bridge...

...Why is this so important?

Luke 7:36-50

FORGIVENESS
1 2 3 4 5 6 7 8 9

Use the code to find a promise to remember!

$\underline{}_5\ \underline{}_1\ \underline{w}_7\ \underline{}_9\ \underline{}_5\ \underline{}_8\ \underline{}_9,\ \underline{h}_7\ \underline{c}_2\ \underline{}_8\ \underline{}_1\ \underline{}_7\ \underline{}_9\ \underline{}_9$ — another word for 'own up'

$\underline{w}_5\ \underline{u}_3$

$\underline{}_1\ \underline{}_2\ \underline{}_3\ \underline{}_4\ \underline{}_5\ \underline{}_6\ \underline{}_7\ \underline{u}_2\ \underline{}_5\ \underline{}_3$

(Look at Psalm 32' to see why it's good to do this!)

1 John 1:9

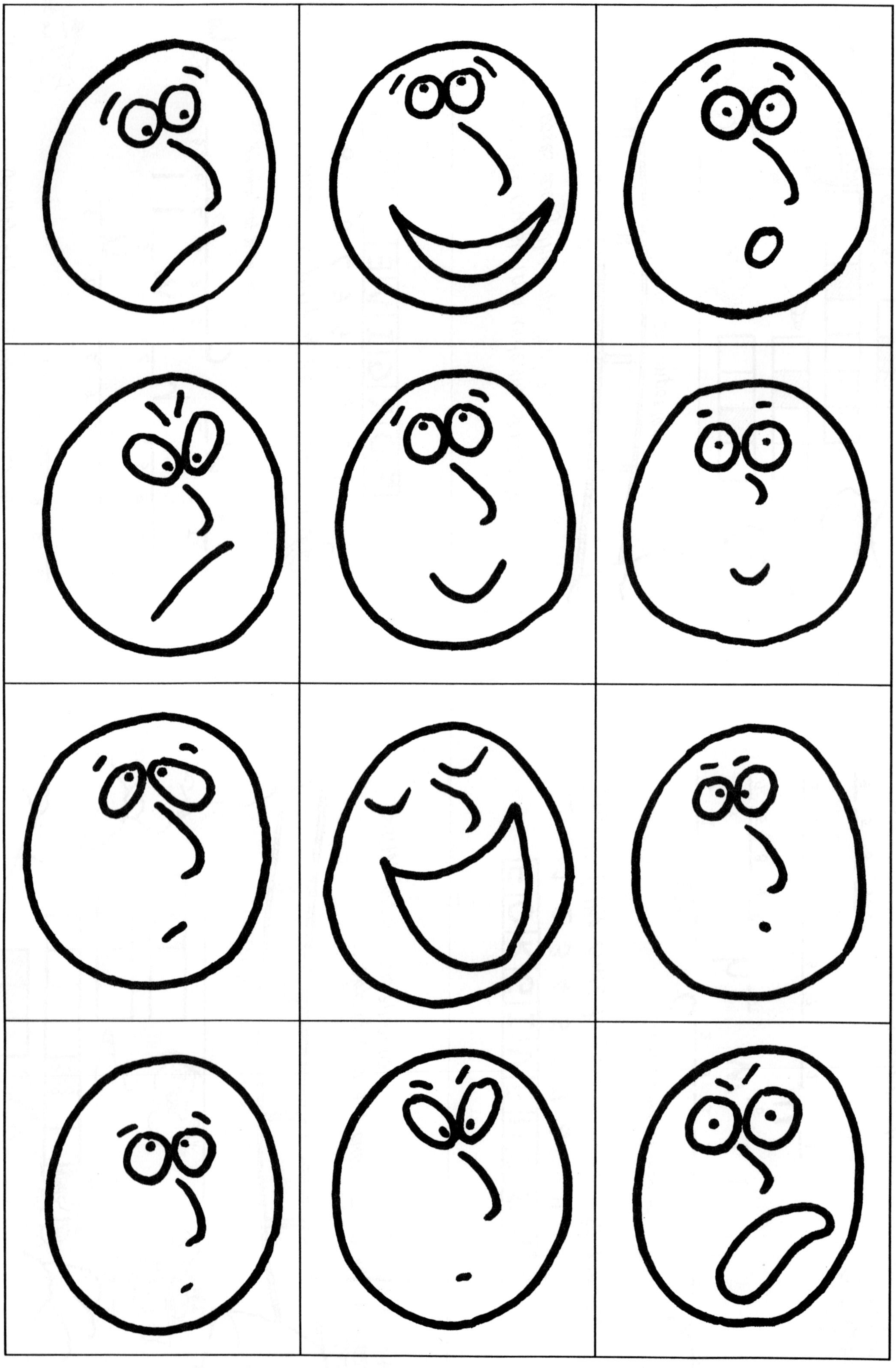

LUKE 7:36-50
- A PARAPHRASE...

[To help your children get involved in these events, this paraphrase has been written in the present tense to give an impression of the story unfolding... The parts between ◄ and ► can be missed out if you wish!

Picture a large room ready for dinner. Jesus is there, but this is not his house - he's a guest of a religious leader (Pharisee), called Simon. There is a table with all sorts of delicious food: roasted meat, freshly-baked bread, fruit....

● *Encourage your children to use their imagination to picture the scene - ask:* **what do you think you could smell? And what do you think you could hear?**

Now picture a woman stepping quietly into the room. She is not one of the guests, but everyone knows who she is: she has a really bad name...

► *Simon's face?* (please see **Option A** on page 86!)

This woman kneels down at Jesus' feet. She begins to cry. She cries so much that her tears flow down onto Jesus' feet. She dries his feet with her hair. Then she kisses his feet and pours perfume on them.

► *The woman's face?*

Simon thinks to himself, "If Jesus were really special, He would know all about this woman! He would never let a woman like this touch him!"

► *Simon's face?*

Jesus knows exactly what Simon is thinking.
   "Simon", says Jesus, ◄*"Imagine two people owe money to the same man. One owes him ten thousand pounds, and the other just a thousand pounds. But neither of them have any money to pay him back.... Now imagine the man tells them both that they don't have to pay him back - not even a penny! Which person will love the man more?"*
   Simon thinks for a moment, then he says, "The one who owed him the most money, I guess."
   "That's right", says Jesus.► "Look at this woman. You did not give me any water to wash my feet after my journey, but she washed my feet with her tears and dried them with her hair. And you did not kiss my face to welcome me, but she has not stopped kissing my feet since she came in. You did not pour oil on my head, but she poured perfume on my feet. The many things she has done wrong have been forgiven, so she wanted to show how thankful she is and how much she loves me."
   Jesus turns to the woman and says, "I've forgiven you for the wrong things you have done."

► *Jesus' face?*

The other guests begin to mutter to each other, "Who does he think he is, forgiving other people for the things they have done wrong?"

► *The guests' faces?*

Then Jesus says, "Because you believe in me, you have been saved from the things you have done wrong. Go in peace."

► *The woman's face?*

9 jesus

LEADERS OVERVIEW

By every swimming pool, lake or waterway hangs a lifebelt in case of emergency: it will fit anyone, reach anyone and remains unsinkable and totally reliable. And the attached rope plays a crucial part in any successful rescue.

When Jesus prayed in the Garden of Gethsemane, he committed himself to doing God's will, even though he knew that this would involve his arrest, trial and crucifixion. Like the rope on a lifebelt, that prayer launched the crucial final phase of God's rescue plan for all people.

Let's do all we can to help each of our children grasp this for themselves!

Jesus died for us. PRAY for each child in your group by name: that he/she will really understand this. And use one of Paul's prayers: "I pray to God that (...) every person listening to me today would be saved..." [Acts 26:29]

We Would Like Our Children to...

... see that Jesus completed a rescue plan; accepting His love and forgiveness is the basis of a new life in relationship with God!

Key Verse

God has made you his friends through Christ's death.
Colossians 1:22

Bible Base

Matthew 26:36-46
(Jesus Prays Alone)

Crucial!

Set the Scene

In advance, find a true *or* fictional rescue story from a video *or* book *or* audio cassette *or* computer game!

1. Show **or** tell the story (**or** have your children play the computer game!).

2. **Either** altogether **or** in small groups, talk together about this and other rescue situations with questions such as:

   ➤ *What do you think would have happened if (name of the rescuer) had not come to the rescue?*

   [Bring out the urgency of the rescue situation: the person might have been seriously hurt... and he/she was probably unable to do anything to help him/herself!]

   ➤ *Was (name of the rescuer) brave to carry out the rescue?*

   [Highlight any danger faced by the rescuer.]

   And if you have time, ask:

   ➤ *Have you ever rescued anyone (or anything!)? What happened?*

   ➤ *Have you ever had to be rescued yourself? What happened?*

   ...and so on.

3. Sum up and move on...

You will need:
to find a rescue story

Present the Bible Base

Option A: Brief Overview

In advance, organise five children *and/or* leaders to act as five 'eye-witnesses' - JOHN, PETER, A JEWISH LEADER, MARY and MARY MAGDALENE. Make a copy of page 102 and give each part to the right person! Also, prepare the visual aid as follows:

1) cut five arc shapes from paper *or* card using the template on the next page;

2) **write** prayed, all alone, badly treated, killed **and** alive again! clearly on the separate arc shapes;

3) if possible, also find five objects to represent the five stages of the story, (eg some greenery for the Garden of Gethsemane, a coin for the betrayal, a thorny branch for the trial, a nail for the crucifixion, a stone for the empty tomb.)

4) give each 'eye-witness' the parts of the visual aid (and object) which go with his/her part of the story.

You will need:
to organise the 'eye-witnesses'
to prepare the visual aid
Blu-tack

You may need:
additional props!

96

1. Station the five 'eye-witnesses' around your meeting room...

2. ...Move around the room as a whole group, stopping to hear each bit of the story - collect the parts of the visual aid (and objects) as you go!

   [If this is impractical in your group, perhaps have your children sitting in a circle with the 'eye-witnesses' scattered among them.]

3. If you have time, use the objects to help your children re-tell the story.

Option B: The Bigger Picture

In advance, find a presentation of the whole Easter story appropriate to your children, (eg a video _or_ paraphrase from a children's Bible, _or_ consider using C S Lewis' *Narnia* stories). Also, prepare the visual aid, as described in 1) and 2) on the previous page.

Simply present the story! Tack the five parts of the visual aid up on a board **or** wall as you go along.

Focus...

In advance, work out what you are going to say at point 3 below!

1. Arrange the five arcs into a cross shape **or** see if your children can do this!

2. Now say something like: **'when Jesus died on the cross, He carried out a rescue plan for all people...'** Rearrange the five arcs into a lifebelt shape **or** see if your children can do this!

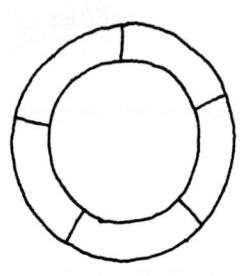

3. Bring out the key points of God's rescue plan. The basic outline below assumes your children have not yet made a decision to follow Jesus, so adapt it as necessary!

   - Remind your children about what God has done as you have prayed throughout this series - be specific! Say something like: **'isn't He kind? isn't He good? isn't He powerful? wouldn't it be great to really get to know Him...?'**

   - Add something like: **'we shouldn't just pray when we want something... that would be 'using' God! God wants the best for us - that's a friendship with Him which we stick at!'**

   cont'd.....

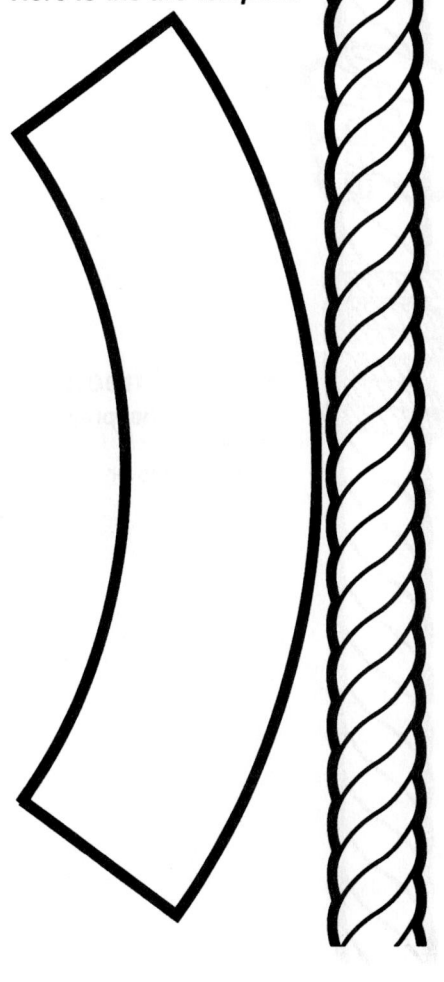

You will need:
to organise this!
to prepare the visual aid
Blu-tack

You will need:
to prepare this!

Here is the arc template

- *'...there is only one way to have this friendship - and that's to be rescued!! (We might not feel like we need to be rescued, but things must be bad if Jesus had to die to save us...)'*

  [Link back to SET THE SCENE, if appropriate.]

- Explain simply and clearly what we need to do to 'be rescued'...

Pray!

In advance, choose carefully <u>how</u> you want to pray from LEARNING TO PRAY on pages vii to x - not all of them will be appropriate here! Also, ask some of your co-leaders to come prepared to talk and pray with children who want to know more... And perhaps get hold of some suitable booklets (eg *Father God, I Wonder* (Kingsway), *God's Friends* (Scripture Union)).

1. Say something like: *'God is offering you friendship through Jesus... what are you going to say to Him - "yes, please"? "no, thanks"? "I need some time to think about it"?'*

2. **NOW PRAY!** Using the idea you have chosen from pages vii to x, simply give your children the chance to talk with God about what they have heard - be sensitive to what God is doing...

3. Also, offer a clear opportunity for your children to talk with a leader one-on-one...

   [Please check the guidelines on praying alone with a child on page vii.]

   ...and be aware that some children may go away and take these steps some time later...

You will need:
to prepare your co-leaders!

Extra Teaching

Prayer Notes

In advance, prepare the 'prayer notes' on page 103 - see page 4 for guidance!

1. Give each child one of the folded 'prayer notes'.

2. Ask your children to complete and colour the picture and complete the key verse on the other half of the sheet.

3. Also, ask your children to **think about God's offer of friendship through Jesus...**

4. ...Ask them to write <u>or</u> draw what they want to say to God about it inside their 'prayer notes'.

5. Finally, ask your children to add this session's 'prayer notes' to the rest by threading the string through the two holes and tying it at the front.

You will need:
to prepare the 'prayer notes'
coloured pens <u>or</u> pencils

Quiz

You will need:
to prepare the 'rope'
two inflatable swimming rings (**or** something similar!)

You may need:
small prizes!

In advance, cut twelve different length pieces of string ('rope'). Make small holes in a piece of card and thread the lengths of string ('rope') through, so that about the same amount of each piece is showing from the front!

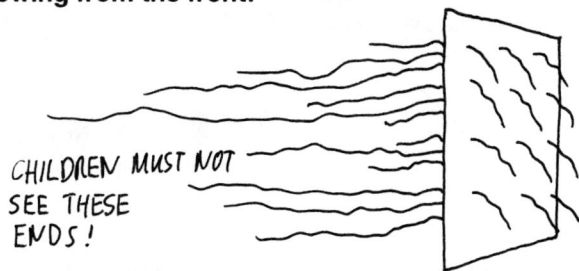

FRONT.

CHILDREN MUST NOT SEE THESE ENDS!

1. Ask your children to get into two teams.

2. Choose one child from each team to be 'rescued'! Position him/her at the same distance from each team - he/she mustn't move from there!

3. Also give each team an inflatable ring ('lifebelt'!).

4. Explain the quiz: *'you have to 'rescue' your team-mate! You will need a 'lifebelt' and 'rope'... to get your 'rope', you will need to answer some questions! For each correct answer, you can choose a piece of 'rope'... tie the first one to the 'lifebelt', then tie the others together. When you think your 'rope' is long enough, hold one end and throw the 'lifebelt' out to your team-mate... if he/she can catch it, the 'rescue' can take place! The first team to do this, wins!'*

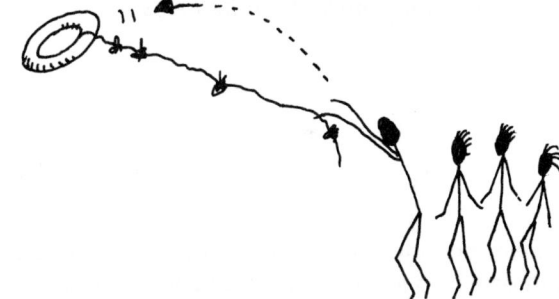

5. Run the quiz, asking the questions on page 104 to each team in turn.

Extra Activities

HOOP-LA

You will need:
for each team of four to six:
a plastic **or** rubber ring (**or** quoit)
string **or** cord
wrapped sweets
a pot **or** container

In advance, tie a length of string *or* cord to each ring.

1. Ask your children to get into groups of about six.

2. Mark a line on the floor and ask everyone to stand behind it... scatter sweets beyond the line.

cont'd.....

3. Give a ring to each group and explain the game: *'see how many sweets you can 'rescue'! Hold on to the end of the string, throw the ring and pull in any sweets inside it. When you 'rescue' a sweet, put it into your team's pot and give the ring to the next person.'*

[Watch carefully to reduce opportunities for cheating!]

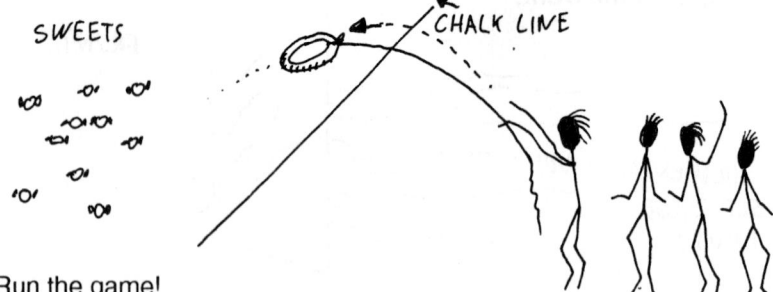

4. Run the game!

5. Share out the sweets at the end.

ALTERNATIVE IDEA:
If you have large hula-hoops, you could play the same game with people instead of sweets!

To Tie This in:

Why did your children want to carry out this 'rescue'? We like sweets! The fact that Jesus wanted to rescue us - and that he was willing to go through so much to carry out the rescue - just shows how much he loves us...!

FRONTIER RESCUE

In advance, choose two different colour balls of wool ('rope') - cut each one into lengths of about 20cms. Also, make two copies of the instructions on page 105.

1. Ask your children to get into two equal-sizes teams...

2. ...Assign an adult leader to each team, and ask each team to choose a child to be its 'captain'.

3. Mark out the playing territory with a clear 'frontier', and a 'base camp' and 'dump' (container) for each team.

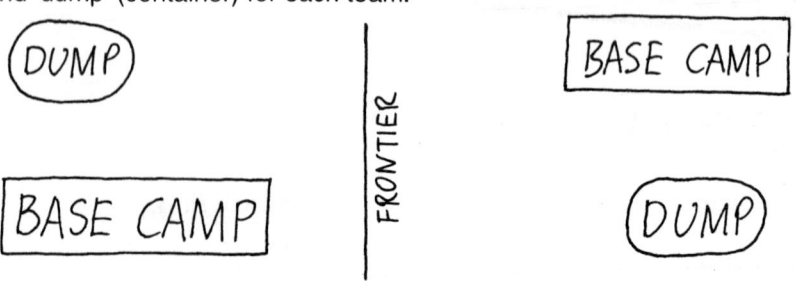

4. Give the adult leader in each team a copy of the instructions and one of the bundles of wool.

You will need:
a lot of space!
to prepare the wool
to make copies
two containers ('dumps')
some way of marking the 'frontier'

You may need:
small prizes!

5. Let each team 'capture' the opposing team's 'captain' and take him/her back to its 'base camp'...
6. ...Once at the 'base camp', allow time for the leader of each team to go through the instructions on page 105 and decide on tactics!

7. Run the game!

To Tie This in:

The 'captain' of each team had to rely on others to be rescued ~ we have to trust in Jesus and what He did on the cross to be rescued! The 'rope' - like prayer - was essential in the rescue. The 'captain' was free once the rescue had taken place ~ we can be freed from sin (wrongdoing) to start a new life in friendship with God Himself.

THE GREATEST RESCUE OF ALL TIME...

You will need:
to organise this!

In advance, think about how your children might like to communicate! Possibilities include:

- designing and drawing a poster *or* a stamp *or*...
- making a radio *or* TV programme;
- writing a newspaper *or* magazine article - with pictures!
- making a booklet;
- writing a song *or* piece of music;
- designing a web-site;
- designing and colouring *or* cross-stitching a card to give to one other person   ...and so on.

Choose as many options as you like, and get together the appropriate materials and equipment!

1. Help your children get excited about what you have been thinking about in this session: the greatest rescue of all time!

2. Then ask: *do you think everyone knows about it? How could we let them know?*

3. Have your children choose from the options available and work out how to tell other people about Jesus' rescue.

4. Have an opportunity to see each one... and could you actually use them to really tell someone outside the group....?

ADDITIONAL IDEAS:

1. Invite someone from a rescue service (eg the fire brigade) to come and talk about their work - highlight the amount of effort that goes into each rescue... link this with all that Jesus went through to rescue us.

2. Arrange for your children to learn some basic lifesaving skills... again, link in with the teaching content, as appropriate.

John:

It was late by the time we finished our meal. We went out into the garden. Everyone was worried, because Jesus said He was going away and leaving us. Then Jesus went away on his own to pray. He was so upset! I heard Him pray, "I'll do what you want me to do, Father..."

Peter:

We must have all fallen asleep. When Jesus woke us up, lots of people were just coming into the garden. Some of them had swords and clubs. And Judas was with them. I didn't understand at first - Judas was one of our group! It turned out that Judas had been given money to help them arrest Jesus. Of course, I tried to stop them. I started to fight, but Jesus told me not to. It was horrible watching Jesus being led away. And later I even let him down myself...

A Jewish Leader:

Late that night, we were called to a special council meeting. Jesus was brought before us. He was accused of all sorts of things I knew he hadn't done! He was beaten and whipped and insulted. Jesus had done nothing wrong! But they still sentenced him to die...

Mary:

I thought my heart would break when I saw Jesus on the cross. Even then, people shouted insults at him. But Jesus just prayed: "Father, forgive them, they don't know what they are doing." When He died, the sun disappeared - it was like the darkest night. Jesus' body was put into a cave-tomb and a huge stone was rolled over the entrance so nobody could get in. Some soldiers came to guard it. Still crying, we went home...

Mary Magdalene:

We went back to the cave-tomb very early on Sunday morning. We were nearly there when the ground began to shake: I was terrified! Then I saw that the stone had been moved and the cave was open again! I was just wondering how that could have happened when I saw an angel, sitting on top of the stone! The angel said: "Don't be scared! You are looking for Jesus... but He isn't here! He has come alive again, just like He said He would!" We ran to tell the other followers. And then we saw Him with our very own eyes! And so did lots of other people.....

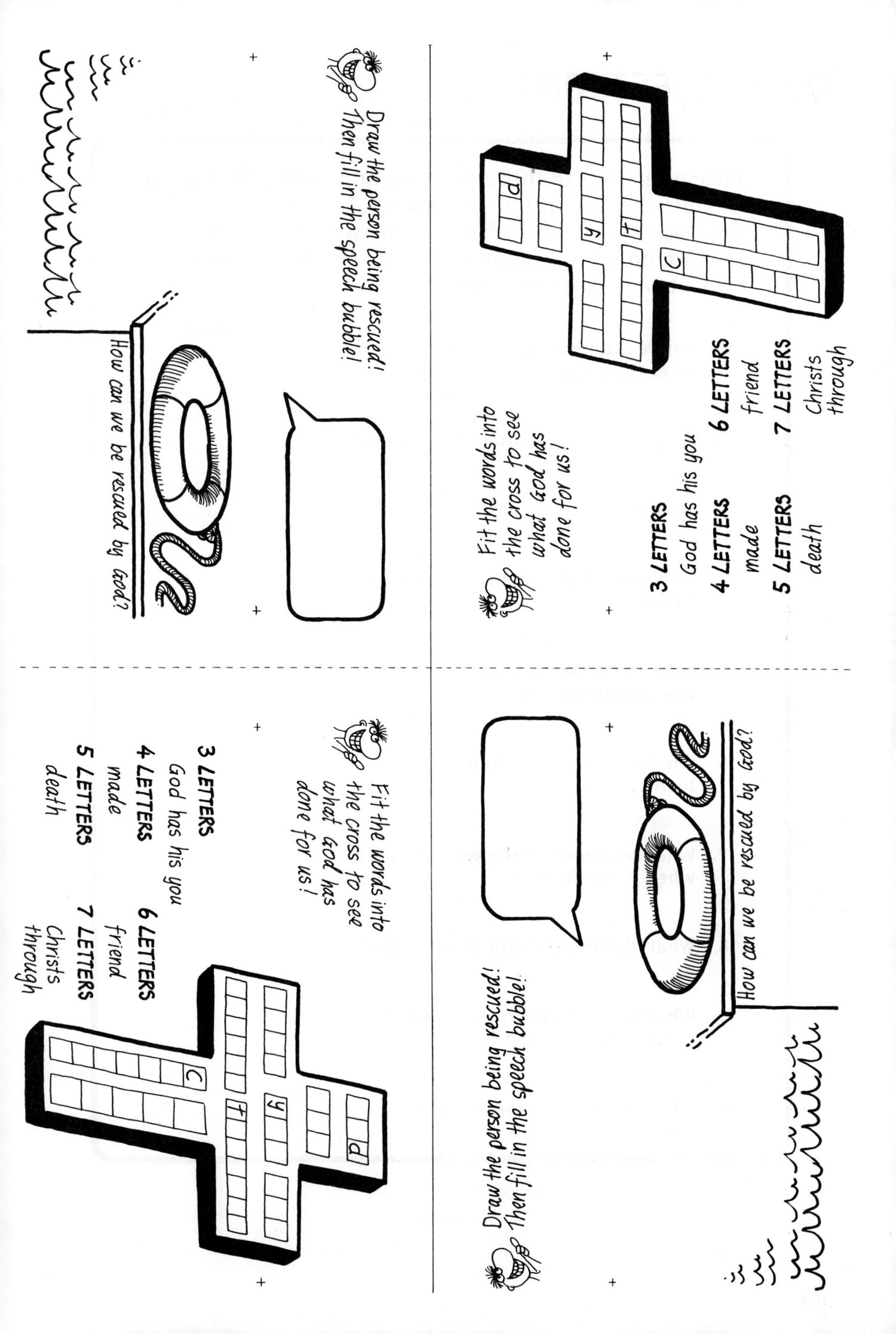

Fit the words into the cross to see what God has done for us!

3 LETTERS
God has his you

4 LETTERS
made

5 LETTERS
death

6 LETTERS
friend

7 LETTERS
Christs through

Draw the person being rescued! Then fill in the speech bubble!

How can we be rescued by God?

QUIZ QUESTIONS

Please read these through in advance and adapt them to suit your children if necessary! Some of the questions have more than one answer, so decide what you are going to accept as correct - children have a very strong sense of fairness!

Your Answers!

1. Where did Jesus and his followers go after their special meal together? _____

2. Why were Jesus' followers worried? _____

3. What did Jesus do in the garden? _____

4. How did the crowd know where to find Jesus? _____

5. How was Jesus treated by the people who arrested him? _____

6. What did Jesus pray when he was being put to death? _____

7. What happened to the whole country when Jesus died? _____

8. What did they do with Jesus' body? _____

9. What did the women see when they went to the cave-tomb? _____

10. Why was the cave-tomb empty? _____

FRONTIER RESCUE

1. Sort your team into *runners* and *stoppers* - have three *runners* for every *stopper* at the beginning, but let children swap roles as the game goes on!

2. Please go through these instructions carefully with your team!

   <u>We have to rescue our captain from the other team's base camp!</u>

   If you are a <u>runner</u>, you are going to take one piece of 'rope' (wool) at a time to our captain. Tell him/her to tie all the pieces of 'rope' together... when he/she has enough to reach over the frontier, the rescue is complete! However, as soon as you cross the frontier into the other team's territory, a stopper from the other team can take your piece of 'rope' from you: If they do this, you too will be imprisoned in their base camp...

   If you are a <u>stopper</u>, you are going to try and stop runners from the other team getting through! If you touch a runner on the arm or shoulder, they have to give you their piece of 'rope'. Bring them back to our base camp and put their piece of 'rope' (wool) into the 'dump'. You cannot capture anyone not carrying 'rope'.

   If <u>runners</u> or <u>stoppers</u> get through to the other team's base camp, you can bring one imprisoned runner back with you.

   If we rescue our captain first, we win!

3. As the game is being played, please make sure that:

   - *runners* only take one piece of 'rope' (wool) at a time;

   - *stoppers* are not rough or inappropriate when they tackle *runners*;

   - the opposing team's *captain* is able to tie together pieces of 'rope' and run them towards the frontier without interference from your team!

   - captured 'rope' is not taken from the 'dump'.

Have Fun!!